Heinrich Heine

Twayne's World Authors Series

Ulrich Weisstein, Editor of German Literature

Indiana University

TWAS 669

Etching by Ludwig Grimm.
Courtesy of the Heinrich Heine Institute in Düsseldorf

Heinrich Heine

By Hanna Spencer

The University of Western Ontario

Twayne Publishers • *Boston*

Heinrich Heine

Hanna Spencer

Copyright © 1982 by G.K. Hall & Company
All Rights Reserved
Published by Twayne Publishers
A Division of G. K. Hall & Company
70 Lincoln Street
Boston, Massachusetts 02111

Book Production by John Amburg

Book Design by Barbara Anderson

Printed on permanent/durable acid-free
paper and bound in the United States of
America.

**Library of Congress Cataloging in
Publication Data**

Spencer, Hanna.
Heinrich Heine.

(Twayne's world authors series; TWAS
669)
Bibliography: p. 160
Includes index.
1. Heine, Heinrich, 1797–1856——
Criticism and interpretation.
I. Title. II. Series.
PT2340.S64 1982 831'.7 82-9310
ISBN 0-8057-6516-6   AACR2

Contents

About the Author

Preface

Chronology

> *Chapter One*
> Biographical Background   1
>
> *Chapter Two*
> *Book of Songs*   12
>
> *Chapter Three*
> *Travel Sketches*   31
>
> *Chapter Four*
> Reports and Essays   44
>
> *Chapter Five*
> Experiments in Fiction   64
>
> *Chapter Six*
> The Mock Epics   73
>
> *Chapter Seven*
> The Later Poetry   94
>
> *Chapter Eight*
> Legacy and Aftermath   141

Notes and References   151

Selected Bibliography   160

Index   167

About the Author

Hanna Spencer (née Fischl) is Professor Emeritus at the University of Western Ontario. She was born and educated in Czechoslovakia where she received the Ph.D. in Germanic and Slavonic languages and literatures from the University of Prague. Professor Spencer emigrated to Canada in 1939, and since 1959, she has been a member of the German Department of the University of Western Ontario in London, Canada. Her publications, written in English and in German, are on the cultural integration of the "New Europe" and on Heine: *Heinrich Heine: Dichter, Denker, Journalist,* (Bern, 1977); and, as coeditor, *Heinrich Heine, Dimensionen seines Wirkens* (Bonn, 1979).

Preface

Heinrich Heine has long been famous as the romantic poet of bittersweet love songs. His *Buch der Lieder* is the most popular book of German poetry—perhaps the most widely circulated book of poetry in all literature—and some of his poems, in the settings of Schubert, Schumann, Mendelssohn, and others, have literally circled the globe "on wings of song." But the response to Heine, the irreverent satirist, provocative social commentator, and brilliant and penetrating essayist whose critique of religion forms an important link in the evolution and revolution of nineteenth-century thought, has been anything but unanimous. Highly acclaimed abroad, he was considered an abomination in his native Germany—except for a relatively small circle of intellectuals who actually read his prose and profoundly appreciated and admired it.

A veritable Heine renaissance began approximately twenty-five years ago with the approach of the one hundredth anniversary of his death in 1956. West Germany, intent on reestablishing its place in the community of civilized nations, could point to Heine as an early spokesman for social justice, democratic freedom, and better understanding between the Germans and the French. East Germans hailed him as a friend of Karl Marx and an early champion of their cause. New trends in literary criticism caused scholars to focus on his writings rather than on biographical trivia and traits of his intriguing, supposedly frivolous, maverick personality and led to a fuller understanding, if not entirely new perception, of his work. Behind the humor and whimsy, readers found an unsuspected substance, lucidity, and coherence of thought, and were struck by his shrewd analyses and at times prophetic insights. Above all, they recognized in him one who experienced some of the very dilemmas which we tend to think of as uniquely twentieth century and who articulated them with extraordinary wit and poignancy.

In my study I begin with biographical aspects and group the works according to genres. However, this plan is modified in places because, in Heine's case, a consistent separation of biographical and literary matters is not only difficult to achieve but is not advisable. The story of his life is mainly one of his fortunes and tribulations as a writer. What excitement or interest his biography holds derives from the particular quality of his writing and the public's response to it. The provocative nature of his writing led to his difficulties with the authorities, family, and colleagues, his exile, and even his marriage. On the other hand, seemingly important events—his travels, for instance, or even his final illness—are significant mainly because of the manner in which they are reflected in his writing. Nor can his prose be comfortably categorized with regard to conventional genres: its blend of reportage, essay, fiction, and autobiography constitutes, after all, its characteristic feature and Heine's unique contribution. Moreover, since changing personal and political circumstances brought about a reversal of Heine's views and attitudes in certain respects, the chronology and biographical context of his oeuvre need to be kept in mind, lest he appear more of a paradox and maverick than he actually was.

Accordingly, the opening biographical chapter will concentrate on Heine's life up to his move to Paris while some of the salient aspects of his later years are mentioned in conjunction with his literary output. The discussion of his poetry is divided into two chapters, to be found at the beginning and end of the monograph. Not to do so would have meant dealing with the *Romanzero* in the beginning or with *Buch der Lieder* at the end, neither of which seemed a desirable option. Thus, this study follows Heine's development, dealing first with the poems and travel sketches of his German period, then with the reflective essays of his prime, and eventually returning, as he did in his later years, to verse.

Needless to say, only a handful of Heine's approximately seven hundred poems could be sampled in this monograph, and the choice was often difficult, especially from among the many exquisite and moving mature poems; in the case of the earlier ones, given the kind of renown the *Buch der Lieder* enjoys, it seemed best to focus on the most popular pieces. As for the prose, the decision on what constitutes Heine's major contributions is somewhat easier—which is not to say that there are not many gems among the miscellaneous minor essays, or to deny that the journalistic reports abound with interesting observations and fascinating, memorable formulations.

In order to reduce the number of footnotes, Heine quotations are identified in the text. These references are based on *Werke und Briefe,* edited by Hans Kaufmann in 10 volumes. Poetry is cited in the original, followed by a strictly literal translation. Prose passages are for the most part given in English, excepting a few instances where the German text is quoted to provide samples of Heine's prose style.

Hanna Spencer

The University of Western Ontario

Chronology

1797   December 13, Heinrich Heine born in Düsseldorf, son of Samson Heine and Betty (née Peira van Geldern).

1807–1814   Attends lycée in Düsseldorf, run by Catholic priests.

1815   Apprentice with banker Rindskopf in Frankfurt.

1817   Goes to Hamburg to work for the firm of his uncle Salomon Heine. In love with cousin Amalia Heine.

1818   His uncle sets him up in business but he fails.

1819   Enrolls at the recently founded University of Bonn; studies under A. W. Schlegel.

1820   Transfers to Göttingen; expelled (January 23, 1821) for involvement in a duel.

1821–1823   Continues studies at Berlin. Frequents salon of Rahel Varnhagen. Active member of Society for Culture and Science of the Jews. Hears Hegel.

1821   *Gedichte.*

1822   *Briefe aus Berlin* appear in newspapers.

1824   Returns to Göttingen University. Hike through the Harz Mountains. Meets Goethe. Writes *Harzreise* and begins *Rabbi von Bacharach.*

1825   June 28, baptized in Heiligenstadt by Lutheran pastor Grimm. July, receives his doctorate in law. Lives with parents at Luneburg. Visits Hamburg and Norderney.

1826–1827   *Reisebilder,* vols. 1–2.

1827   April–August, visits England. September, coeditor of Cotta's *Neue Allgemeine Politische Annalen* in Munich. October, *Buch der Lieder.*

1828   Journey to Italy. Father dies.

1830   Sojourn in Hamburg; visits Helgoland.

1830–1831 *Reisebilder,* vols. 3–4.

1831 May 1, arrives in Paris. Correspondent for *Augsburg Allgemeine Zeitung.*

1834 *Salon,* vols. 1–2. Meets Crescence Eugénie Mirat (Mathilde).

1835 German Federal Assembly bans Heine's writings.

1836 Granted pension from French Government (until 1848).

1837 *Salon,* vol. 3.

1840 *Ludwig Börne.* Resumes reports for *Augsburg Allgemeine Zeitung* (till 1843). *Salon,* vol. 4.

1841 Marries Mathilde. Duel with Salomon Strauss. Begins work on *Atta Troll.*

1843 Meets Karl Marx in Paris. Visits Hamburg.

1844 Second journey to Hamburg. Writes *Deutschland. Ein Wintermärchen. Neue Gedichte.* Uncle Salomon dies. Beginning of inheritance feud.

1847 Ballet scenarios. *Atta Troll. Ein Sommernachtstraum* published in book form.

1848 Physical breakdown.

1851 *Romanzero.*

1853 *Vermischte Schriften.*

1855 Friendship with Elise Krinitz (La Mouche).

1856 Heine dies on February 17 and is buried on Montmartre.

Chapter One
Biographical Background

Heinrich Heine lived in an age of upheaval. Born eight years after the French Revolution of 1789, Heine outlived by eight years the revolution of 1848 which sent Metternich, staunch defender of the old order, fleeing to England. He was a child when Napoleon conquered Europe. As a youth he witnessed the wars of liberation and, in the aftermath of the Congress of Vienna, the restoration of the old regimes under the aegis of the Holy Alliance. He was in his prime when the Paris July Revolution of 1830, which brought the Citizen-King Louis Philippe to the throne, sent shock waves through Europe, and he was one of those who exuberantly hailed the event as proof that bloodless reform is possible. In a Europe where absolute monarchs still clung to their "divinely ordained" power, revolution, in the eyes of Heine and his like-minded contemporaries, meant the practical application of the recently proclaimed rights of man. Specifically, it meant the struggle for constitutions which would provide parliamentary government and civil liberty—in Heine's words the "emancipation of mankind."

Because Heine was a Jew, the idea of emancipation had an added significance. The discriminatory treatment of European Jewry is a matter of record. Jews were not allowed to own landed property, were barred from public posts and from most trades and professions, were subject to special taxation, and, in big cities, were forced to live in ghettoes. But these and other legal and material restrictions were of course just the tip of the iceberg. Even more insidious were the less tangible ways in which anti-Semitism affected its victims. And although Heine, in childhood and later in life, may have been spared the shock of direct persecution, he remained aware of the stigma as well as the bond of his Jewishness. Doubtless it contributed to his extraordinary sensitivity to the portents and practical implications of ideas.

Düsseldorf, where he spent the first seventeen years of his life, had no ghetto and members of the Heine family associated freely with their Catholic neighbors. In fact, since the region (Jülich-Berg) of which

Düsseldorf was the capital was for thirteen years under French adminis-
tration, the Jews in this area felt for a time the beneficial influence of the
French Revolution: The provisions of the Napoleonic code granted
them rights of citizenship and equality before the law. However, after
Napoleon's defeat the Duchy of Berg was ceded to Prussia, and the Jews
were returned to their inferior status. No wonder that Heine was a
lifelong admirer of Napoleon! He saw in him—as did Goethe—the
larger-then-life genius and regarded him, up to the "18th Brumaire"[1]
at any rate, as the champion and continuator of the Revolution. And he
never tired of ridiculing Prussia, epitome of the militaristic, autocratic,
dull-witted oppressor.

Heine's boyhood seems to have been happy and serene. He later
spoke of his deep love for his easygoing, charming father, a rather
ineffectual businessman whose textile firm eventually went bankrupt.
It was his mother, Betty van Geldern, daughter of a respected physician
and herself well educated, who ambitiously directed the education of
their four children: Harry—his original name—Charlotte, Gustav, and
Maximilian. In view of the independent attitude which her eldest son
subsequently displayed in matters of religion, it is of interest that she
considered herself religiously emancipated, an "enlightened" deist who
looked to human reason and morality as guiding forces. So compelling
was her rationalist conviction that she even endeavored to shield her
children against the realm of fantasy by disallowing visits to the theater,
the reading of novels, and the telling of ghost stories.

The Rhineland was predominantly Catholic, and Harry was educated in the Lyceum which was then housed in a Franciscan monastery.
He was to cherish affectionate memories of some of his Jesuit teachers,
especially Rector Schallmeyer who introduced him to philosophy. Thus
Heine was exposed in his formative years to a mixture of traditions:
Jewish and Christian, German and French, rationalist and orthodox.
As well, he grew up in a region whose political fortunes were closely
linked to the changing tides of European history. Whatever the impact
of these conditioning factors—which, after all, were similarly valid for
countless contemporaries—overriding them all was his unique and
mysterious genius.

The urge to write verse surfaced in his early teens. When we first hear
his voice, in a letter from Hamburg to his school friend Christian Sethe,
the conviction that he is above all a poet seems firmly established in his

mind. The work of his pen and his image as a writer were to remain his foremost concerns throughout his life, sustaining him even during the eight agonizing years of terminal illness, literally to his last breath. But first he had to serve another apprenticeship. At age eighteen, he was introduced to the world of business. In preparation for the commercial career which his parents had in mind for him, he was sent as a trainee to a firm in Frankfurt and then to Hamburg, where his uncle Salomon Heine, a wealthy and influential banker, was to make a businessman of him. Needless to say, the undertaking failed completely. Amid the hardheaded, parvenu business circles of one of the most active mercantile centers in Germany where banking, one of the new institutions of capitalism, played a pivotal role, the young poet felt isolated and miserable. It was a matter of hate at first sight. In his uncle's fashionable circle he was the poor and somewhat gauche country cousin, yet felt superior in intelligence and sensitivity. "In Hamburg war es mein einzig Pläsir, dass ich mir besser vorkam als alle anderen" ("In Hamburg, my only amusement consisted in thinking myself better than everyone else"),[2] he was later to recollect. At the time, however, he took himself more seriously: "Whores aplenty but no muses," he reports in his first letter to Sethe.[3] From the very beginning of his stay, he cast himself in the role of a free and natural poet (*frei und unbefangen*) in a world of Philistines.

Moreover, he promptly fell in love with his cousin Amalia. In fact, judging from the same letter, he had already decided that "Molly," whom he had last seen when she was fourteen, would be his source of inspiration: "Rejoice, rejoice: in four weeks I shall see Molly. With her, my muse will return. I have not seen her in two years." One letter and three-and-a-half months later—two months after Molly presumably appeared on the scene—he can already announce to the same correspondent: "Sie liebt mich *nicht*" ("She does not love me") and expand on the "infernal pain" which this discovery brings.[4] The particular doom of exclusion which Heine suspects for himself will henceforth remain one of his pervasive themes.

Biographers have expended much effort in probing Heine's actual feelings toward Amalia and her younger sister Therese who, they thought, was his muse number two after Amalia married in 1821. Rather more to the point is the observation that Heine became infatuated with love itself, or, more accurately, with unrequited love; and that he managed to make the lovesick lament, through endless variations, into an archsymbol, encompassing infinite possibilities of the sense of exclusion and all the shades and stages of pain which a passionate heart suffers in a hostile or indifferent world. The tragic, tender, and lonely persona at the center of Heine's lyrical poetry, though a construct of his imagination and not to be equated with his real self—as he himself repeatedly warned—has nevertheless acquired a life of its own which has fascinated generation after generation of readers and with which young lovers of all ages have identified.

In the course of the three years he spent in Hamburg, young Harry Heine so convincingly demonstrated his lack of interest in and aptitude for a business career that the family gave him permission to take up the study of law, and Uncle Salomon agreed to subsidize him. This grudgingly granted support ("if only the silly boy had learned something, he would not have to write books") was to last, albeit intermittently, throughout the poet's life. His love-hate relationship with his wealthy uncle was as ambivalent as that with his publisher, Julius Campe. Heine was actually one of the first German authors who attempted to make a living by his pen, and consequently he was never free of financial worries. (The German term *freier Schriftsteller* is patently a misnomer!) It irked him to have to wrangle and quibble continuously about money and sometimes, as he put it, even to beg; and he alternately resented and appreciated the two men on whose good will he depended. Campe ultimately offered more than financial survival. The connection with him in time became the all-important link to the German public and, in a sense, the link between the author and his life's work; which helps to explain why the letters to Campe make up such a large part of Heine's correspondence from Paris.

But to return to the student who in 1819 enrolled in the recently founded University of Bonn. Although jurisprudence was to be his field, Heine took up mainly literary and historical subjects and plunged wholeheartedly into student activities—even joining a fraternity.[5] Among his teachers in Bonn was August Wilhelm Schlegel, the preeminent authority in matters of prosody and metrics. The young poet showed him some of his efforts, and received valuable advice and encouragement. Fifteen years later, he would present him as a tragicomic figure and make him the target of merciless and cruel ridicule, but we can be certain that he owed to Schlegel's tutelage much of his concern with prosodic detail and his appreciation of the importance of form.

After two semesters in Bonn, he transferred to Göttingen in order to concentrate on his legal studies. (It was usual to change universities, and the custom to study at more than one prevailed in Germany until fairly recently.) But his stay in Göttingen turned out to be shorter than planned. "Rusticated" (suspended for a term) because of his involvement in a duel, he moved to Berlin. There, a whole new world opened to him. Unlike Bonn and Göttingen or even Hamburg, Berlin was a metropolitan center. Shortly after his arrival, Heine was befriended by Varnhagen and Rahel von Ense, in whose literary salon he soon became a frequent and welcome guest. Varnhagen, a liberal aristocrat, and his Jewish wife were enthusiastic Goethe fans. They proved to be intelligent and perceptive critics whose judgment Heine valued. Rahel died in 1833 but Varnhagen remained one of Heine's most loyal supporters who stood by him on many an occasion when the author was embroiled in controversy.

For a time, Heine was also involved in the Verein für Kultur und Wissenschaft der Juden, a society for the cultural emancipation of the Jews, of which Eduard Gans was the principal promoter. But the poet's most important contact and teacher in Berlin unquestionably was Georg Wilhelm Friedrich Hegel, from whom he took lectures and whom, through the Varnhagens, he also met personally.

Opinion among Heine scholars is divided as to how much of Hegel's philosophy Heine actually absorbed and understood.[6] However, Heine was without a doubt one of the first to have recognized, in the notoriously impenetrable web of Hegel's prose, the radical implications of the philosopher's thought. He perceived Hegel to be fundamentally a rebel, at a time when the philosopher appeared to be a servile upholder of Prussian authoritarianism and was in fact highly respected by the powers-that-be. (Tongue in cheek, Heine later asserted that Hegel deliberately obscured his radicalism through the rhetoric of his convoluted prose.) He was profoundly impressed by the Hegelian notion that "facts are 'merely' the result of ideas." From Hegel, he took over the glorification of the historical process and the concept of the history of ideas, especially the notion of the progression from religion to philosophy, and the view that the "spirit of the age" represents the pertinent developmental stage of the human mind writ large. (The poem "Bergidylle," included in *Buch der Lieder,* already contains these views in a nutshell.)

It is a moot question whether Heine's preference for antithetical formulations was intensified by his exposure to Hegel, in whose philosophy the opposition of thesis and antithesis figures so prominently. In Heine's world view antithetical thinking was to be similarly conspicuous, and throughout his work he was to rely on the exploitation of contrasts and to show his penchant for setting up opposing frames of reference in order to emphasize a point.

Hegel's influence later was augmented and reinforced by Saint-Simonian ideas. But whatever was taken over from Hegel, from Saint-Simon's disciple Prosper Enfantin (or, for that matter, from innumerable others, for Heine's memory seems to have been as retentive as a sponge, even though not always accurate), his genius blended it all in a highly original way and produced results entirely his own.

Eventually, Heine returned to Göttingen to complete his doctorate in law. But he knew that his diploma alone would not suffice to get him the career in university or public service to which he ardently aspired. Four weeks before he was to receive his degree, on June 28, 1825, he presented himself to the Lutheran Pastor Grimm in Heiligenstadt to be baptized. The baptismal certificate was needed, as he put it, as his *Entréebillet zur europäischen Kultur* ("Entry ticket to European culture"). He pretended to make light of it by placing the blame on Napoleon's geography teacher who "had failed to inform his pupil that Moscow was very cold in winter."[7] Harry Heine became Heinrich Heine, at least to posterity: he preferred to sign himself "H. Heine." To call the events a "conversion" would, however, be an overstatement. No change of view or commitment was involved and he regretted the step almost at once. In time, he came to feel the sting of humiliation all the more when he realized that baptism had been of no avail, either in helping him to attain a position or in "washing off" his Jewishness.

There followed an interlude of travel, not so much the classical "grand tour" as a period of seemingly restless meandering between his parents' home in Lüneburg, Hamburg, and Norderney, where he sought relief from his persistent headaches. He was, of course, writing. "Die Harzreise" [Journey through the Harz] had already appeared in a journal and created a considerable stir. Soon two volumes of *Reisebilder* [Travel Sketches] were to be published by Hoffmann und Campe and bring their author instant fame and notoriety. But in spite of the doctoral diploma, the baptismal certificate, and Varnhagen's warm letters of recommendation, his search for congenial employment that would ensure his financial independence proved unsuccessful. Then, in May, 1827, an attractive proposal—indeed the only job offer he was ever to receive—reached him during a sojourn in England. Baron Johann Friedrich von Cotta, the noted liberal-minded publisher of Goethe and Schiller, invited him to Munich to be coeditor of a new journal, *Politische Annalen*. It was not a demanding job since the actual editorial work was to be in the hands of Dr. Friedrich Ludwig Lindner, and it paid the comfortable salary of 2,000 gulden a year. One would assume that Heine should have been delighted. Instead, he accepted this seemingly ideal offer only reluctantly and took his time in journeying to Munich, pausing for several lengthy visits along the way. He looked up former associates in Göttingen, stopped in Kassel to meet Jakob and Wilhelm Grimm, and lingered long enough to have his portrait painted by Ludwig Grimm. (The result was the well-known profile which shows him in a Byronic pose.) He took a detour to Frankfurt to spend a few days with Ludwig Börne, then the foremost political writer in Germany, and visited his brother Max who was a medical student at Heidelberg. There, the author of the "subversive" *Reisebilder* was taken into custody and unceremoniously escorted out of the Kingdom of Württemberg. This incident (about which Heine himself remained strangely silent) is indicative of his notoriety even at this early stage of his career; it also illustrates the oppressive attitudes then prevailing in Metternich's Europe.

When he finally arrived in Munich in November, 1827, Heine was willing to commit himself only for six months. In retrospect, it is obvious that his heart was not in this assignment. While the few pieces he contributed to the journal were written in his usual brilliant prose, his tone was uncharacteristically cautious and mild: The position which he really wanted was a professorial appointment at the University of Munich. But to qualify, the candidate had to be acceptable to the Bavarian court. In the words of a recent biographer, "it may seem strange to us that he would think that he would be in a better position as a professor by the grace of the King of Bavaria than as an editor in the house of Cotta; but apparently he did think so."[8]

Confident about his prospects of receiving the appointment for which, he knew, he had been recommended by the influential Minister of the Interior Eduard von Schenk, he resigned from his editorial post

and departed for Italy. His journey took him across the Brenner Pass, to
Verona, Milan, Genoa, and Florence; that he appeared to be following
in Goethe's footsteps probably was no coincidence. However, unlike his
illustrious model, he did not head for Rome but remained in Northern
Italy—perhaps because, throughout his journey, he expected word of
his Munich appointment. He waited in vain. Instead, he subsequently
learned that the man who was being installed in the professorial chair
was Hans Ferdinand Massmann. The "teutomaniac" Massmann was to
become one of Heine's favorite and most enduring butts of ridicule.

The trauma of this disappointment was intensified by the news,
which caught up with him just then, that his father had died. Heine
felt profoundly dejected and uncertain where he might settle. His
mother now lived in Hamburg, completely dependent on Uncle Salomon. It was there that Heine returned after trips to Potsdam and
Helgoland. In the meantime, the Italian sketches had appeared in print
and the ensuing uproar over the author's vitriolic attack on the poet
August von Platen (whom he suspected of having helped block the
Munich appointment) left him beleaguered and isolated.

Such was Heine's mood when the news of the Paris July Revolution
reached Helgoland, where he was vacationing. Like many other European liberals, Heine was elated, and at once returned to Hamburg
where, rumor had it, the tricolors were flying and the Marseillaise was
resounding in the streets. But Hamburg had barely even heard the
news; and when, three weeks later, some unrest did develop, it took the
form of anti-Semitic demonstrations. Heine now began to think seriously about moving to Paris, while at the same time trying once more
to establish himself in Germany. He was still dreaming of an academic
post, this time in Berlin or Vienna, and when Varnhagen convinced
him that his hopes were naive, he solicited recommendations support-
ing him for the position of Ratssyndikus (a counsel, or solicitor, for the
municipal government) in the city of Hamburg. Needless to say,
nothing came of it.

More and more, France looked like the "Promised Land." "Yes, I
repeat," Heine exclaimed at the conclusion of *Reisebilder,* "Freedom is a
new religion, the religion of our time. . . . The French are the chosen
people of this religion, in their language the new gospel and dogma has
first been recorded, Paris is the New Jerusalem and the Rhine is the
Jordan which separates the sacred land from the country of the Philis-

tines" (3:488). A few months after he wrote this, in May, 1831, Heine moved to Paris, where he was to spend the rest of his life. Salomon Heine financed the journey and promised a continuing subsidy.

What made Paris seem a "New Jerusalem" was the fact that the Bourbon Charles X had been dethroned and replaced, without bloodshed, by the "Citizen-King" Louis Philippe of Orleans. To those who welcomed this coup as an epochal event[9]—and no one did so more exuberantly than Heine—it was the fulfillment of the liberal's ultimate dream: an elected king, a victory for the little people, a revolution without terror.

But Heine had another, possibly even more compelling reason to look upon Paris as an ideal haven. It was the center of the Saint-Simonian movement.[10] Its founder Claude Henri Count Saint-Simon had died in 1825, reportedly with the words on his lips "l'avenir est à nous" ("the future belongs to us"). Three years later, his ideas of a classless utopian society based on moral-religious renewal began to gain followers. His disciples envisioned a modern industrial society, organized and led by scientific experts for the good of all. There was to be no exploitation or inherited privilege, vested power was to be abolished, and rewards made commensurate with talent and merit. Marriage was declared obsolete and equality of opportunity extended to women. Saint-Simonians believed in the reinstatement of sensuality and dreamed of a society founded on love, justice, and beauty. They postulated not merely a new economic and social order but a new religion, a veritable church with an authoritarian hierarchy led by a *Père Suprême*, a "supreme father." The role of this "pope" was filled by Barthélemy Prosper Enfantin. For about ten years the movement attracted considerable attention, eventually turning into a bizarre cult that mixed radicalism with autocracy.

Many features of the Saint-Simonian "doctrine" must have had great appeal for Heine, who first learned of it in Germany, while trying in vain to establish himself in a job that would offer some measure of financial independence and social status. The Saint-Simonians' rejection of privilege by right of birth, their affirmation of man's physical needs—not excluding sexual ones—their appreciation of intellectual superiority, and, above all, their regard for the artist, deeply impressed Heine, as evidenced in various mysterious allusions to the impending renewal of mankind. "Paris is not merely the capital of France, but of the whole civilized world," he wrote in 1832; "a new art, a new religion, a new life is being created here" (4:413f.).

A new life it had indeed turned out to be. The *Globe,* mouthpiece of the Saint-Simonians, announced on May 22, 1831, the arrival in Paris two days earlier of "Dr. Heine, the famous German author . . . one of those courageous men who stand up for the cause of progress." Soon Heine found himself appreciated, even sought after as a celebrity and accepted in the most sophisticated and influential circles of French society. Whereas in Germany he had waited in vain for an acknowledgment by Tieck, Uhland, or Goethe of having received his book of poetry, he was able, in due course, to count among his friends and acquaintances Victor Hugo, Honoré de Balzac, George Sand, Théophile Gautier, Gérard de Nerval, Alfred de Musset, Alexandre Dumas, Hector Berlioz, Vincenzo Bellini, Frédéric Chopin, Franz Liszt, the Rothschilds, and influential politicians.

Heine's move did not constitute a break with his German public. But his role now changed from that of an outsider, a rejected lover, and irreverent wanderer, to that of a defender of the cause of emancipation and of an intermediary between Germany and France. However, the voluntary exile in the course of time turned into a painfully irreversible one, after his works—along with those of other so-called Jungdeutsche—were banned by the German diet and a warrant was issued against him in Prussia. (Heine claimed that it was renewed every Christmas, along with the Christmas lights.) After an absence of twelve years, he ventured to return to Hamburg nevertheless, to see his mother again, to talk with his publisher, and to present his wife to the family.

Crescence Eugènie Mirat (whom he called Mathilde because "Crescence scratched his throat") had been his mistress and companion since 1834. He had met her when she was a nineteen-year-old salesgirl in her aunt's Paris shop. Of Belgian peasant background, she was completely uneducated and, despite his efforts, she remained so. According to Heine, she was even unaware that he was a famous German poet. But she was vivacious and attractive, and by most accounts theirs was a happy, though often stormy, relationship. They reportedly fought and squabbled like little children but also cared for each other with real affection. To provide for Mathilde financially beyond his own lifetime was one of Heine's central concerns. It was in fact the reason for legalizing their relationship, after they had lived together for seven years, when he was about to fight a duel. This duel with Salomon Strauss had been brought about by certain passages in his book about Ludwig Börne.[11] Once again, as on several other occasions, purely private aspects of Heine's life were inextricably bound up with his record as a writer. Indeed, anything that really mattered to him invariably had to do with the work or self-image of the poet, and the story of his remaining years turns out to be the story of his tribulations as a writer and a record of his publications. An unpleasant inheritance feud after the death of Uncle Salomon (involving a legacy for himself and security for Mathilde) is believed to have hastened Heine's physical collapse. The dispute arose because of the family's fear of what he might divulge about them in his memoirs, and resulted in their attempt to apply a censorship of sorts to what he might write. Even the awful eight years of terminal illness are remarkable mainly because he coped with his agony by writing immortal verse almost to the last hour.

Heine was fifty nine when he died in February, 1856, yet his image lives on as that of a young man. According to his wish, he was buried on Montmartre, without a religious ceremony. For his epitaph he had suggested a simple statement: "Here lies a German poet."

Chapter Two
Book of Songs

The collection through which Heine's poems have achieved this world renown, entitled simply and appropriately *Buch der Lieder* [Book of Songs], was published by Hoffmann und Campe in Hamburg in 1827. The book contains poems Heine wrote beginning at age sixteen, although the majority originated between 1821 and 1824, that is, two to five years after he had left Hamburg and his muse. It is divided in chronological order into sections entitled "Junge Leiden" [Young Sorrows], "Lyrisches Intermezzo" [Lyric Intermezzo], "Heimkehr" [Homecoming], "Aus der Harzreise" [Songs from the Harz-Journey], and two sections called "Nordsee" [North Sea].

The book first attracted only moderate attention, but from 1837 onward its popularity soared. In its thirteenth edition at the time of the author's death, *Buch der Lieder* became the most widely read book of poetry in world literature, establishing the fame of its author and the wealth of its publisher, to whom Heine had sold it for a pittance. Indeed, so great was the popularity of *Buch der Lieder* that it overshadowed Heine's other, more mature and superior work, or at least delayed its appreciation. The broad public which the poet of *Buch der Lieder* so successfully wooed would have been shocked and repelled by the views that Heine actually held, while many of those who might have appreciated the more problematic and sophisticated "other" Heine turned away from the poet whose name was synonymous with *Buch der Lieder*.

The format, tone, and style of *Buch der Lieder* is that of the folksong. Despite—or because of—his adherence to the simple forms and metric lines of the conventional four-line stanza, Heine achieved a distinctive voice surprisingly early. For, by and large, Heine's poetry owes much of its unique appeal to the subtle tension and interaction between the seemingly natural, homespun format and the flashes of his agile, sophisticated mind. Still, modern readers of the *Buch der Lieder* may well wonder what captivated the imagination of readers for a century.

They will find in it much that seems mannered and derivative—
especially in the early sections—and throughout, they will encounter
verses that are flawed and weak, glib and trivial, and many that seem
unbearably sentimental. The thought of facing 240 poems of which all
but a handful deal with unrequited love may lead us to ask with Heine,
albeit in a different context than he had in mind:

> Anfangs wollt ich fast verzagen,
> Und ich glaubt, ich trüg es nie;
> Und ich hab es doch getragen—
> Aber fragt mich nur nicht, wie?[1](1:38)

(At first I almost despaired and thought I could not bear it; yet I did—but do
not ask me how.)

Yet when we pause to scrutinize these lines, glib and facile as they seem,
like an entry for an album which, in fact, they originally were, we find
that even they tell us something about Heine's craft. We note the easy
melodious rhythm, the syntactic simplicity along with a talent for the
mot juste: "verzagen" has a certain tentative, poetic flavor; "getragen"
is more subtly effective than the anticipated "ertragen" would have
been; we note the rising crescendo inherent in the second "und"; and,
finally, the turn in the last line when the all-too-easy rhythmic flow is
halted to introduce the suggestive question. Moreover, this poem
achieves a certain poignancy, as the penultimate of nine songs and the
only one compressed into one stanza within a cycle that tells the usual
bittersweet tale. Heine had a knack for arranging his independently
conceived poems so that they complemented and enhanced each other
in content, rhythm, and mood, to form a larger whole.

Early in the *Buch der Lieder,* amid a mixed lot of cliché-ridden tales
which for the most part team love with death, we encounter two ballads
of extraordinary power. "Die Grenadiere" has become an international
favorite in the setting of Robert Schumann in which the strains of the
Marseillaise underscore the climactic ending. But the verses retain their
impact even if one blocks out the memory of Schumann's tune. Two
returning soldiers of Napoleon's defeated Grand Army reveal a simple,
unconditional loyalty to their immortal hero, whose presence shines
through with almost mythic force. It is noteworthy that here, in one of
his first poems, Heine has combined the traditional genre with a topic

of current interest: in 1813—Heine tells us that he wrote the ballad when he was sixteen—Napoleon was still very much in the news. While borrowing from tradition—echoes of the Scotch ballad "Edward" are clearly discernible[2]—Heine already shows his own touch. Such lines as "Der eine sprach: Wie weh wird mir/Wie brennt meine alte Wunde" ("One of them said: oh, what grief comes over me—how my old wound is burning") exemplify his penchant for presenting an abstract concept (grief) through concrete, sensual experience and his skill in making the experience palpable: here, for instance, the alliteration reinforces the semantic content of "weh" and "Wunde."

An even more dazzling example of Heine's early artistry is the ballad "Belsazar," which used to provide a trusty showpiece for recitalists in days long past. The biblical tale of the blasphemous challenge to Jehovah originally is told in the Book of David (V), but it is likely that Heine's immediate source of inspiration was Byron's version of "Belshazzar." Lord Byron, discoverer of new worlds of suffering, was Heine's admired model in many ways. Scene and mood are established with a few strokes, in a perfect blend of sound and sense, starkly contrasting the nocturnal stillness in the town below with the riotous goings-on in the king's palace. Note the verbal economy which is maintained throughout the poem:

> Die Mitternacht zog näher schon;
> In stiller Ruh' lag Babylon.
>
> Nur oben in des Königs Schloss,
> Da flackert's, da lärmt des Königs Tross. (1:52)
>
> (Midnight was slowly coming on;
> In silent rest lay Babylon.
>
> But above in the palace of the king,
> There is the blaze of torches and the noise of the king's gang.)

After Belsazar's brazen challenge to Jehovah the tension mounts, beginning with the anxiety that suddenly grips the king himself, followed by the deafening silence of his men and finally, the spine-chilling writing on the wall. By the choice of words and the blend of rhythm, image, and sound the poet does not so much describe as physically reproduce the scene. The hand really appears and writes on the wall:

Doch kaum das grause Wort verklang,
Dem König ward's heimlich im Busen bang.

Das gellende Lachen verstummte zumal;
Es wurde leichenstill im Saal.

Und sieh! und sieh! an weisser Wand
Da kam's hervor wie Menschenhand;

Und schrieb, und schrieb an weisser Wand
Buchstaben von Feuer, und schrieb und schwand. (1:53)

(No sooner was the gruesome word spoken
When the king's heart secretly filled with dread.

The shrill laughter suddenly stopped;
Deadly silence filled the hall.

Behold, behold! On the white wall
A thing appeared like a human hand;

And wrote and wrote on the white wall
Letters of fire, and wrote and was gone.)

In contrast to the biblical source as well as to Byron's poem, both of
which dwell on the interpretation of the Mene Tekel, Heine invented
his own ending, a "man-made" ending so to speak, leaving the reader to
ponder its implications with regard to human relations: "Belsazar ward
aber in selbiger Nacht / Von seinen Knechten umgebracht" ("Belsazar,
however, in the selfsame night / was put to death by his own horde").
According to Heine's own recollection, this ballad was also written
when he was not quite sixteen. And it may or may not be a coincidence
that the topic anticipates Heine's later concerns and his announcement,
in quite different tones, of the death of Jehovah.

With "Lyrisches Intermezzo" and "Heimkehr" we come to the
poems with which Heine's name is most commonly identified. Here he
developed some of his most characteristic features: his flair for epi-
grammatic brevity and suggestive terseness that leaves room for the
reader's imagination, his vivid imagery, his musical phrasing, his
unexpected ironic turns and brilliant quips. Among these poems we
find many of Heine's most renowned gems. In all the world's literature,

they have invited the greatest number of musical settings; of the approximately five thousand songs that have been made of Heine's poems, the majority by far is based on verses from the middle period of *Buch der Lieder,* pieces which he wrote when he was between twenty-four and twenty-seven years of age.

Heine never made a secret of the care and deliberation that went into his work. Yet the very charm of his poetic style lies in its seeming artlessness and easy grace. His language flows so naturally that the meaning rather than the binding meter appears to dictate the word order. Rhyme and meter do not seem strained or restraining but have a heightening effect. In his best pieces, each line is a perfect blend of content and expression, and with their melodious cadences the words themselves seem to make music. Take, for example, the poem which opens the cycle, "Intermezzo No. 1":

> Im wunderschönen Monat Mai,
> Als alle Knospen sprangen,
> Da ist in meinem Herzen
> Die Liebe aufgegangen.

> Im wunderschönen Monat Mai,
> Als alle Vögel sangen,
> Da hab ich ihr gestanden
> Mein Sehnen und Verlangen. (1:72)

> (In the lovely month of May
> When all the buds were bursting,
> 'Twas then that in my heart
> Love sprang up.

> In the lovely month of May,
> When all the birds were singing,
> 'Twas then that I confessed to her
> My longing and my yearning.)

The attempt to render this little poem in English makes one realize just how meager is its intellectual content and, conversely, how intricate and magical (pronounce: untranslatable) the fusion of the various lyrical elements which produce its effect. It consists of two sparse quatrains of similar structure, each containing a statement which in turn is made up of two parts. The most obvious feature, shared by the two stanzas, is their first line which sounds like a mellifluous, perhaps somewhat old-fashioned formula—a refrain positioned at the beginning—suggesting the sweetness and recurrent renewal of spring. This seemingly swift-footed tetrameter with masculine ending is followed by three trimetric lines with feminine endings.[3] The resulting effect is a sense of slowing down, of a waiting for something more significant to happen, and the content confirms it: springtime reigns not only outdoors but within the heart of the lyrical "I." The smooth-running phrase is filled with meaning, and the general, natural phenomenon is transformed into something unique and personal.

But, apart from rhythm and meter, how is this crescendo of feeling achieved? Each of the two stanzas contains a statement about two events which are linked by coincidence. But what the syntax presents as a temporal relationship turns out, by way of image, to be a relationship of another kind. "Als alle Knospen sprangen" ("when all the buds were bursting"): No translation can do justice to the effect of the explosive onomatopoeia (kn, sp, spr, ng) of this line, especially in contrast to the mellow and softly undulating one that preceded it: spring's awakening is physically converted into language. "Da ist in meinem Herzen die Liebe aufgegangen." "Aufgehen" is a rather commonplace word which is used in connection with many things, but "Liebe" ("love") is not one of them: it means "to open" as a door might open, or "to rise" as the sun or dough rises. And it means to come up, as a seedling comes up. Of course, herein lies the creative spark of the poem. Before our mental eye we see the human heart suddenly transform itself into a bud and simultaneously we recognize the heartlike quality of the bursting buds; human love becomes part of a natural, elementary force, participant in the universal rite of spring.

The second quatrain seems to run parallel to the first. Again the alluring phrase rolls prettily along, followed by "als alle Vögel sangen": in context, even this sturdy cliché exudes a childlike simplicity. Again the natural event and the human experience turn out to be not merely simultaneous events but of the same quality. Once again, what is implied is not so much a comparison as an equation. But this time, the equation does not quite balance. Something new is added which introduces the difference between singing creatures and the human lover. The subtle turn occurs with the reference to her ("ihr"). That it takes two to be in love is not much of a novelty. Novel, however, is the manner in which the reference is made, almost inadvertently, through the dative of a pronoun: not as "dir," which the verse would have equally allowed and which would have been the conventional way, but which also—and that is of course the crux of the matter—would have invited this "du" into the poem. No, the focus does not shift even for a moment from the lyrical "I" at its center. What the rhythms and imagery of these two stanzas have led up to, what moreover all the rhymes have prepared us for, is the lover's "Sehnen und Verlangen," which fills the last line and which seems to linger on after the poem has ended.

What began as a celebration of harmonious unity with nature has turned into its opposite, a feeling of loneliness and deprivation in the midst of a blossoming world. There is none of the exuberance that emanates from the passage in Goethe's famous "Mailied":

> O Mädchen, Mädchen
> Wie lieb ich dich
> Wie blinkt dein Auge
> Wie liebst du mich!

(Sweetheart, sweetheart, how I love you! How your eyes shine, how you love me!)

Note that Goethe's joyous declaration was ushered in by a stanza that in essence has the same semantic content as Heine's:

> Es dringen Blüten
> Aus jedem Zweig
> Und tausend Stimmen
> Aus dem Gesträuch

(Buds press forth from every branch and thousand voices [sing out] from the bush).

With Heine, love is never a partnership, never the shared, fulfilling and mutually enriching experience conveyed by Goethe, but it always results in an even deeper isolation. Heine's capacity for inventing different modes of presenting the lament of the aching heart seems inexhaustible. In one of the best known ("Lyrisches Intermezzo No. 33"), the lone pine tree in the barren north yearns for the palm in the distant, torrid south. Besides embodying, to the point of absurdity, hopeless love and extreme isolation, this poem also exemplifies Heine's view of the universe in which Eros reigns supreme:

> Ein Fichtenbaum steht einsam
> Im Norden auf kahler Höh'.
> Ihn schläfert; mit weisser Decke
> Umhüllen ihn Eis und Schnee.
>
> Er träumt von einer Palme,
> Die, fern im Morgenland,
> Einsam und schweigend trauert
> Auf brennender Felsenwand. (1:85)
>
> (A fir-tree stands lonely
> Far north on barren height.
> It drowses; ice and snow
> Envelop it with a white blanket.
>
> It dreams of a palm-tree
> Which far away in the Orient
> Mourns lonely and mute
> On a sunparched cliff.)

Instead of the parodies which this pining pine tree and the silently mourning palm would seem to invite, numerous imitations have been stimulated by it and it provided the lyrics for no less than 121 musical settings.[4] It is, by the way, one of the few poems which objectivizes the theme without the presence of the lyrical "I." This is also true in the case of the lotus flower in love with the moon ("Lyrisches Intermezzo No. 10"). Prompted by the information that the lotus closes its bloom in sunlight, Heine depicts her dreamily awaiting her lover the moon, being awakened by him, and revealing her "friendly" beauty to his sight, and finally, in an even more suggestive third stanza, glowing and trembling with desire. Such are the purely tonal effects of these lines that even a reader who knows no German will appreciate its sensuality:

> Sie blüht und glüht und leuchtet,
> Und starret stumm in die Höh';

Sie duftet und weinet und zittert
Vor Liebe und Liebesweh. (1:76)

(She blooms and glows and shines
And silently gazes upward;
Full of fragrance, she weeps and trembles
With love and loving woe.)

To present the female as the loving partner is not exactly Heine's habit, and even in this instance the point of view is not really that of a woman: clearly the lotus flower, paragon of purity, modesty, and beauty yet exuding affectionate devotion and exotic sensuousness, is the product of a man's wishful thinking. For Heine, it is almost always the man who is endowed with a passionate heart, while the object of his longing and cause of his perennial grief and frustration is the distant, heartless, inscrutable beauty. She is a Sphinx, a vampire, a marble statue, a siren. She is the "Loreley."

The poem which popularly goes by this name, "No. 2" in the cycle "Heimkehr" (where it appears untitled), has, in the setting of Friedrich Silcher, achieved the status of a folksong comparable to Goethe's "Heidenröslein" (or in English to Robert Burns's "Auld lang syne"). It is so beloved and so much felt to be part of German folksong heritage that even in Hitler's Germany, when the name of the Jew Heine was unmentionable, the "Loreley" could not be left out of songbooks. It was accompanied by the note "author unknown." How Heine would have savored the irony of it all as well as the implicit compliment!

"Lureley," meaning "elfin rock," was the name associated with a cliff in the Rhine valley (between Bingen and Koblenz) in the vicinity of some hazardous reefs. Clemens Brentano had transformed it into "Lore Lay" and given the name to a woman whose tragic death near the treacherous rock he described in a ballad of that name. Other contemporary poets picked up the theme, among them Joseph von Eichendorff, who in "Waldgespräch" made her into a demonic wood nymph, and Count Otto Heinrich von Loeben, whose ballad "Der Lurleyfels" thematically is very similar to Heine's. Anyone interested in comparing two treatments of essentially the same subject, one eminently forgettable and the other a masterpiece, should read Count Loeben's "Der Lurleyfels" and compare it with Heine's poem, which runs:

Ich weiss nicht, was soll es bedeuten,
Dass ich so traurig bin;
Ein Märchen aus alten Zeiten,
Das kommt mir nicht aus dem Sinn.

Die Luft ist kühl und es dunkelt,
Und ruhig fliesst der Rhein;
Der Gipfel des Berges funkelt
Im Abendsonnenschein.

Die schönste Jungfrau sitzet
Dort oben wunderbar,
Ihr goldnes Geschmeide blitzet,
Sie kämmt ihr goldenes Haar.

Sie kämmt es mit goldenem Kamme,
Und singt ein Lied dabei;
Dat hat eine wundersame,
Gewaltige Melodei.

Den Schiffer im kleinen Schiffe
Ergreift es mit wildem Weh;
Er schaut nicht die Felsenriffe,
Er schaut nur hinauf in die Höh.

Ich glaube, die Wellen verschlingen
Am Ende Schiffer und Kahn;
Und das hat mit ihrem Singen
Die Loreley getan. (1:103)

(I don't know what it means that I am so sad; I can't get out of my mind a tale
from olden times. The air is cool and it is growing dark, and the Rhine flows
peacefully; the peak of the mountain sparkles in the evening sunshine. The
fairest maiden sits up there, wonderfully, her golden jewelry glitters, she
combs her golden hair. She combs it with a golden comb, and sings a song
the while; it has a wondrous, powerful melody. The boatman in his little
boat is seized with wild woe; he does not see the rocky reefs, he only looks up
to the heights. I believe the waves finally swallow the boatman and his boat;
and that the Loreley has done with her singing.)

Even without the sentimental strains of Silcher's tune, the words seem to sing. The trimetric lines with crossed rhymes, feminine cadenzas alternating with masculine ones, make up six quatrains, each of which forms a closed unit—with the exception of the two middle ones which, not accidentally, belong together. Throughout, structural elements seem to fuse perfectly and naturally with image and sound, each stanza weaving its own particular spell. In the first it is mainly the broken syntactical awkwardness which reinforces the vague melancholy and groping uncertainty evoked by the haunting memory of "ein Märchen aus uralten Zeiten." Next, the view shifts from the subjective mood, the mindscape, to the external scene. Twilight is descending on the calmly flowing river. The uncertain rhythm gives way to smoothly flowing lines which, with their dark vowels, physically convey what the words say, finally coming to rest on the one majestic noun that almost takes up the whole last line of the stanza: "Abendsonnenschein." With this our gaze has lifted to perceive "die schönste Jungfrau." Having somehow materialized out of the glowing radiance, she unmistakably sits there, triply endowed with objects of gold as befits the fairytale figure, all three of them—jewels, hair, and comb—feminine attributes that are now brought into play in a stunningly simple, commonplace, and yet exquisitely feminine act: the lady combs her hair. The reiteration, "Sie kämmt es mit goldenem Kamme," leads into the next stanza and thus into the siren's song. Moreover, it underscores the repetitive quality of the stroking motion itself, with the hint of hypnotic fascination and sexual lure, at the same time connoting narcissistic aloofness. Similarly evocative are the allusions to the song itself. Presently the view is again lowered to the river, to show the devastating effect of it all on the man in the small boat who is now mentioned for the first time. The circle is finally completed with the return to the "I" with which it began: "Ich glaube die Wellen verschlingen." The initial question has been answered, and the haunting tale has been recreated, as it were, before our eyes. Only at the very end does the spell receive a name, and the untitled poem the title under which it was to be remembered, making Loreley an archetype of the forever elusive one whose beauty is matched by the coldness, if not the evil, within.

Break of Mood

Heine's talent for establishing mood with a few vivid strokes was matched only by his flair for breaking it. The sudden change of mood became a characteristic feature of the *Buch der Lieder*, known as *Stimmungsbrechung*. In its early form it had ensued from the dream situation, when fantasy inevitably ended with a return to reality. But from *Lyrisches Intermezzo* onward, this awakening takes on many guises that are symptomatic of that tension between nostalgia and disillusion, romantic sentiment and critical judgment, emotion and intellect which inform Heine's entire work and being. In effect it usually means that his sense of humor asserts itself. Readers come to expect the tongue-in-cheek punch lines and ironic reversals as quintessential Heine. It should be noted that Heine's irony does not fall into the category of "Romantic irony" associated with other poets of the era. Unlike the ironic flights of the Romantics which allow them to escape from reality, Heine's irony has precisely the opposite effect; it bursts the idealistic bubble by confrontation with reality:

> Die Jahre kommen und gehen,
> Geschlechter steigen ins Grab,
> Doch nimmer vergeht die Liebe,
> Die ich im Herzen hab.

> Nur einmal noch möcht ich dich sehen,
> Und sinken vor dir aufs Knie,
> Und sterbend zu dir sprechen:
> "Madame, ich liebe Sie!" (1:117; "Die Heimkehr, No. 25")

> (The years keep coming and going,
> Generations pass to the grave,
> But never the love will perish
> Which in my heart I have.

> Just once more I'd like to see you
> And sink upon my knee
> And speak to you while dying:
> "Madame, ich liebe Sie.")

What prompts the reader's chuckle in the first place is of course the deflating last line with its startling shift—a linguistic shift that cannot be duplicated in English—from the intimate *du* of the first seven lines to the tamely formal address of "Madame" with *Sie* instead of the climax which we were led to expect. This shift in speech levels denotes the incongruity between the grandiloquently idealized "eternal" passion and the rather mannered and lean relationship on which it had fed, revealing a world of difference between illusion and reality. In presenting this love in such obviously hyperbolic terms, Heine exposes its hollow bathos and histrionic posturing. In mocking maudlin sentiment, he mocks not only contemporary poetic trends but also himself.

Ein Jüngling liebt ein Mädchen,
Die hat einen andern erwählt,
Der andre liebt eine andre,
Und hat sich mit dieser vermählt.

Das Mädchen heiratet aus Ärger
Den ersten besten Mann,
Der ihr in den Weg gelaufen;
Der Jüngling ist übel dran.

Es ist eine alte Geschichte,
Doch bleibt sie immer neu;
Und wem sie just passieret,
Dem bricht das Herz entzwei. (1:88; "Lyrisches Intermezzo, No. 39")

(A young man loves a girl
Who has chosen another;
This other one loves another
And has married her.

The girl in vexation
Marries the first man
Who comes her way;
The young man is up against it.

It is an old story,
But it remains ever new;
And when it happens to someone
His heart breaks.)

The *Stimmungsbrechung* in this poem has a diametrically opposite effect. Here the unadorned summary of the plain facts, the cheerfully galloping meter, the colloquial idiom and carefree tone, all combine to make light of the old predicament—up to the last two lines, that is, when the right of feeling is reaffirmed.

Heine's touch can at times be so subtle that the ironic undertones may be—and indeed have been—overlooked. In pieces that nineteenth-century readers (including the composers) took at face value, modern readers can frequently savor an ironic intent and sophistication that eluded his contemporaries. To give just one example: I am convinced that poem "No. 14" in "Die Heimkehr," "Das Meer erglänzte weit hinaus" [The sea shone far into the distance], which sounds hopelessly maudlin when taken literally, actually contains a parodistic inversion of Goethe's ballad "Der Fischer" to which its second stanza unmistakably alludes. (Compare: "Der Nebel stieg, das Wasser schwoll". . . "Aus deinen Augen, liebevoll", and the reference to a "Fischerhaus" in the beginning.) Both poems involve a man by the water's edge and a "damp lady" that draws him to his watery doom. But the fatal waters in the peculiarly Heinesque version flow from the lady's eyes. Does he mean to provide a more realistic interpretation of the liquid element's demonic power?

A return visit to Hamburg in 1823 inspired one of the key poems of the cycle "Die Heimkehr," about the man who visits the deserted house of his former beloved. It is a powerful poem about suffering revisited, embodied in his agonizing former self, the man shut out from love and home whom the lyrical "I" encounters under his sweetheart's window. The concept of the divided self does not, of course, originate with Heine. "Zwei Seelen wohnen, ach, in meiner Brust" ("Two souls, alas! dwell in my breast"), Goethe had said in *Faust,* and in the Romantic era the theme of the double was a familiar one, notably in the formulation of E. T. A. Hoffmann, from whom Heine may have borrowed the image of the ghostlike companion. But it was probably Heine's poem, unforgettably set to music by Franz Schubert, which gave the term "Doppelgänger" European currency.

> Still ist die Nacht, es ruhen die Gassen,
> In diesem Hause wohnte mein Schatz;
> Sie hat schon längst die Stadt verlassen,
> Doch steht noch das Haus auf demselben Platz.

Da steht auch ein Mensch und starrt in die Höhe,
Und ringt die Hände, vor Schmerzensgewalt;
Mir graust es, wenn ich sein Antlitz sehe—
Der Mond zeigt mir meine eigne Gestalt.

Du Doppelgänger! du bleicher Geselle!
Was äffst du nach mein Liebesleid,
Das mich gequält auf dieser Stelle,
So manche Nacht, in alter Zeit? (1:115; "Die Heimkehr, No. 20")

(The night is still, the streets are at rest,
My darling used to live in this house;
She has long since left town,
But the house still stands in the same place.

A man stands there too and stares up,
And wrings his hands in agony;
I shudder when I see his face—
The moon shows me my own features.

You double-ganger! pale fellow!
Why do you ape my love-pain
Which tormented me in this very place
On so many a night in times gone by?)

"North Sea"

Reading *Buch der Lieder* today, one cannot help but marvel at this
amazing phenomenon of thematic monotony—the critic Gerhard Storz
calls it "monstrous"[5]—coupled with such a seemingly inexhaustible
wealth of variations. Each poem a self-contained unit, almost always
bound internally by finely wrought antithesis, yet all of them, by clever
arrangement, bonded together through links of association or contrast.
One of the early pieces is about *Minnesänger*, the medieval troubadours.
Clearly, this is a label Heine wished to apply to himself—he actually
did so in his letters—thus placing his preoccupation with Eros into an
ancient and highly respected European tradition.[6] Still, no one was
more aware of the ridiculousness of the eternal love plaint than the poet
himself.

"Teurer Freund! Was soll es nützen,
Stets das alte Lied zu leiern?
Willst du ewig brütend sitzen
Auf den alten Liebeseiern?

Ach! das ist ein ewig Gattern,
Aus den Schalen kriechen Küchlein,
Und sie piepsen und sie flattern,
Und du sperrst sie in ein Büchlein." (1:127)

("Dear friend! What use is it
To grind out the same old tune?
Do you want to go on hatching
Those old love-eggs?

What a never ending clucking!
Out of the shells crawl little chicks
And they chirp and they flutter
And you lock them into a little book".)

Even within the *Buch der Lieder* one can discern Heine's progressive attempts to free himself from the shackles of the love theme and the format of the folksong. One new concern which begins to emerge in the longer poems that follow "Die Heimkehr"—a concern which will assume great prominence in his later opus—has to do with religion. "Donna Clara" is a biting satire on anti-Semitism. When his friends found this poem amusing, the poet expressed surprise: he, for once, was not amused. More or less oblique allusions to the topic of religion are also contained in "Götterdämmerung" [Twilight of the Gods], "Almansor," "Die Wallfahrt nach Kevlaar" [Pilgrimage to Kevlaar], and, most explicitly, "Bergidylle" [Mountain Idyll].

The breakthrough in content and form which Heine evidently sought was achieved in a cycle of twenty-two poems entitled "Die Nordsee" [North Sea] which makes up the last part of *Buch der Lieder*. They are rhapsodic hymns that were inspired by the poet's encounters with the sea. (Beginning in 1823, as already mentioned, he vacationed on the isle of Norderney to cure his headaches.) But the thematic focus on the seascape was novel not only for Heine: it is said that he "discovered" the sea for German literature, much as Albrecht Haller had discovered the majesty of the Alps.

The experience of the ocean's elemental power, grandeur, and beauty seems to have opened fresh perspectives and vistas and unleashed an exuberant surge of feeling in Heine. Others made use of free verse before him. Klopstock's famed odes had been succeeded (and surpassed) by the hymnic masterpieces of the young Goethe, and in Heine's own time Ludwig Tieck brought free verse into vogue. Yet once again Heine develops a distinctive note. In his inimitable way he uses the freedom of free verse to create rhythmic and tonal effects that sensually convey the ebb and flow, the roar and music of the surf. In marked contrast to the simple idiom of his folksongs, he now produces high-flown rhetoric and compounds descriptive epithets with a Homeric ring, in line with the mythological topics which he introduces. It is mythology with a difference, however, as Heine presents his own irreverent interpretation of the familiar classical figures. His deities of antiquity do not stand for eternal and universal absolutes—quite the opposite. He shows them as exiles, deposed and replaced by Christian gods (the plural is his), and he means to infer the relative and changing validity of all religious "truths." One of the key poems which makes this point explicit is entitled "Die Götter Griechenlands" [The Gods of Greece] and uses Schiller's poem of the same title as point of reference and departure.

The hymnic tone does not preclude the use of *Stimmungsbrechung* or the treatment of humorous and even burlesque topics. In fact, just as some of Heine's seemingly simple songs achieve their particular piquancy by sophisticated nuances, so the exalted format when superimposed on commonplace topics produces hilarious effects, which were not appreciated by all of Heine's readers.

Throughout these poems, one can hear and feel the sea, not by itself but always in relation to the reflecting, questing man at the center whose loneliness and vulnerability (and sometimes fatuity) it throws into relief:

Fragen

Am Meer, am wüsten, nächtlichen Meer
Steht ein Jüngling-Mann,
Die Brust voll Wehmut, das Haupt voll Zweifel,
Und mit düstern Lippen fragt er die Wogen:

"O löst mir das Rätsel des Lebens,
Das qualvoll uralte Rätsel,
Worüber schon manche Häupter gegrübelt,
Häupter in Hieroglyphenmützen,
Häupter in Turban und schwarzem Barett,
Perückenhäupter und tausend andre
Arme, schwitzende Menschenhäupter—
Sagt mir, was bedeutet der Mensch?
Woher ist er kommen? Wo geht er hin?
Wer wohnt dort oben auf goldenen Sternen?"

Es murmeln die Wogen ihr ew'ges Gemurmel,
Es wehet der Wind, es fliehen die Wolken,
Es blinken die Sterne, gleichgültig und kalt,
Und ein Narr wartet auf Antwort. (1:207)

Questions

The sea, the midnight, the desolate sea
Where a young man stands,
His head full of doubts, his breast of sorrows,
And with bitter lips he questions the ocean:

"O solve me the riddle of being,
The painful, primordial riddle,
Whereover so many heads have been cudgelled,
Heads in hieroglyphic bonnets,
Heads in turbans and scullcaps of black,
And heads in perukes, a thousand other
Heads of poor men who drudged and sweated—
Tell me, what purpose has man?
From whence does he come here? And whither goes?
Who lives above there, beyond where the stars shine?"

The billows are murmuring their unending murmur,
The breezes are blowing, the cloudbanks are flying,
The stars are blinking, indifferent and cold,
And a fool awaits his answer.[7]

In 1827, Heine was glad to have found in Hoffmann und Campe a
publisher who was willing to bring out in one book all the poems that

had been published here and there, in the volume *Gedichte,* in journals, as a "lyrical interlude" between the tragedies *William Ratcliff* and *Almansor* (which, for all the energy, enthusiasm, and hope he invested in them, never did catch on), or in the two volumes of *Reisebilder* [Travel Sketches]. And Heine must have actually meant it when he supposed that his poems "would now sail into the sea of oblivion,"[8] for he was willing to forego any honorarium or royalties (Campe, in fact, paid him fifty Louis d'or by canceling a debt). He lived to experience his world fame as the poet of the *Buch der Lieder,* with translations into many languages. It was the first German book to be translated into Japanese—comparable to *Werther*'s translation into Chinese, a parallel which did not escape Heine's notice. But at the time of its publication, he believed that he had done with lyrical poetry and that his strength and his mission lay elsewhere. He had established himself as a successful, albeit controversial, author of brilliant, scintillating, challenging prose.

Chapter Three
Travel Sketches

In striking contrast to the litany of lament that dominates the songs, a profusion of topics awaits the reader of *Reisebilder* [Travel Sketches]. Indeed, the agility with which the author moves from topic to topic constitutes one of the book's outstanding features. Eventually, as Heine's mature poetry becomes more varied and provocative, this curious disparity between his poetry and prose will disappear. But during the first decade of his career, Heine seems to place poetry and prose in separate compartments. He refers to poetry—even though it is of vital importance to him—as "schöne Nebensache," beautiful but inconsequential. In his prose, which he writes more or less concurrently, he shows himself acutely aware of belonging and contributing to a critical period of history: from the beginning, his prose attests to his wide range of interests in social and political matters and to his critical, quizzical mind. The prose author presents himself as "Mann der Idee . . . der Bewegung" ("man of the idea, the movement"), meaning one who is sensitive to the movement of history, and he is proud of his unique ability to decipher *die Signatur des Geistes* ("the signature of the spirit of time"). (These notions have a distinctly Hegelian ring.)

Moreover, if creativity consists in seeing the connection between things that ordinarily are not connected, in recognizing a similarity of phenomena where none had been noted before, Heine is endowed with it to an exceptional degree. His rare talent of picking something familiar and, with a flash of imagination and wit, giving it a fresh meaning, turns his *Travel Sketches* into intriguing and charming journeys of discovery.

The genre did not, of course, originate with Heine. The structure of the journey has an ancient tradition, from the *Odyssey* to the picaresque novel and Laurence Sterne's *Sentimental Journey*; and travelogues were much in fashion in Heine's time. He himself referred to his *Harzreise* as a "mixture of nature description, wit, poetry and observation à la Washington Irving."[1] His pieces nevertheless had the impact of novelty. Their originality lies in their grace, in the sparkling yet transparent prose, the penetrating comment, the sharp eye for detail, the deadly accuracy of satire, and, throughout, the spell of an unrivaled sense of humor. But their paramount innovation consists in the interlacing of narrative elements with descriptions, reflections, anecdotes, dialogue, and poetry.

Heine has actually produced a synthetic construct, a unique collage. The reaction of his contemporaries ranged from delight in the stimulating potpourri to bewilderment and even dismay because these pieces clearly were not "organically grown," which was then deemed a criterion of a respectable work of art. Even critics who were favorably inclined, and who looked in vain for some sort of "inner unity," were content to pronounce that the unity of the *Reisebilder* derives from, and resides in, the author's idiosyncratic viewpoint, in his impressionistic outlook. Although such opinions have been voiced until fairly recently,[2] readers of the postexpressionist era, attuned to sophisticated collage techniques and to the manipulation of metaphoric and symbolic elements practiced by modern authors, are better able to discern the fundamental line of thought which binds this seemingly random mix of themes. Moreover, there clearly exists a development, a continuing line which leads from one essay to the next, while at the same time Heine's horizon expands and his comments become more searching and sharply focused.

The Poet and the Philistines

"Die Harzreise" [Journey through the Harz] is the best known by far of Heine's prose works, a high-spirited romp which from its famous first sentence onward maintains a tone of sophomoric irreverence: "Die Stadt Göttingen, berühmt durch ihre Würste und Universität, gehört dem Könige von Hannover und enthält 999 Feuerstellen, diverse Kirchen, eine Entbindungsanstalt, eine Sternwarte, einen Karzer, eine Bibliothek und einen Ratskeller, wo das Bier sehr gut ist" ("The town of Göttingen, famous for its sausages and university, belongs to the king of Hanover and contains 999 dwellings [literally, "fireplaces"], assorted churches, a maternity hospital, an observatory, a lock-up for students, a library, and a rathskeller, where the beer is very good." 3:18).

The theme of this work pivots on the contrast between the stuffy artificiality and narrowness of Göttingen and the carefree exuberance of the poet-traveler who feels the throbbing allure of nature. Based on a hike through the Harz Mountains which Heine made in the autumn of 1824, "Die Harzreise" satirizes the antipoetic, pedantic Philistinism among Göttingen academics, with their deadly urge to classify and categorize, and contrasts it with the wholesome existence of the plain folk who live in harmony with their natural environment. The life of the miners in the Claustal is seen as idyllic, the shepherd is a true king, the miner's daughter and River Ilse are princesses.

This thematic antithesis is incorporated in the structure as well. The stages of the actual journey fill the days while at night, the traveler is haunted by specters of the life he left behind. This alternation of sun-lit adventures with nightmares that unmask the poet's fears is repeated five times. Perhaps the most hilarious of these dreams is the one in Goslar, when the sleeper is visited by the ghost of Dr. Saul Ascher, epitome of a sober rationalist who expounds in Kantian terms the impossibility of the existence of ghosts. (Dr. Ascher was a Kantian scholar whom Heine met in Berlin and who, like some others, has escaped oblivion only because Heine immortalized him in his wit.)

Not all Philistines were left behind in Göttingen, however, and the traveler meets various specimens in the course of his journey. Once his silent devotion before an awesome sunset is interrupted by "Wie ist die Natur doch im allgemeinen so schön!" ("How beautiful is nature in general!" 3:62). "A young merchant" made this inane, off-key exclamation, betraying with one word his pomposity. Philistines lack sensitivity to beauty, to poetry, to nature. Everything is judged from a sober utilitarian, strictly self-centered point of view: trees are green because green is good for the eyes, God created cattle because beef broth is good for you, Spontini's opera has a certain usefulness, since its kettle drums, elephants, trumpets, and tom-toms fuel the military spirit.

Poking fun at Philistines is actually a Romantic legacy. But while the German Romantics applied the term mainly to uncultured nonstudents, Heine takes a more general view and sees them as chief enemies of the poet: humorless, self-satisfied, slaves to routine, opponents of new ideas, narrow-minded enemies of enlightenment. Through Matthew Arnold's famous essay which introduced Heine to English readers and laid the basis for his legendary fame in mid-Victorian

England, the term Philistinism was popularized in the English speaking world with the connotation that Heine had given it.[3]

Heine's hiking tour in 1824 actually led to Weimar where he called on Goethe; more accurately, where he had been granted an audience by Goethe. However, the account of the trip—to which Heine liked to refer as a "fragment"—breaks off before he reaches Weimar.

Heine's ambivalent relationship to Goethe has been the topic of much analysis.[4] Goethe represented the acknowledged apex of German literature. He was the revered eminence, "Wolfgang Apollo" as Heine called him, a legend in his own time with whom all aspiring poets somehow had to reckon. As a twenty-four-year-old student Heine had approached him for the first time by sending him a copy of his little book *Gedichte* (1821), accompanied by a fawning dedication: "I love you. . . . I kiss the holy hand which has shown me and the whole German people the way to heaven. . . ."[5] Such extravagant adulation is indicative of the treatment to which Goethe appears to have been accustomed. He did not respond, nor did he acknowledge the receipt of the tragedies *Almansor* and *William Ratcliff* which Heine sent him two years later. This time the tone of the covering note was more restrained.[6]

That the interview turned out to be a disappointing, if not downright traumatic experience may be surmised from the silence which followed it. (However aloof or patronizing Goethe may have been, one suspects that Heine was not proud of his own performance either; his flippant reports about the conversation are of a much later date.) Not only is there no reference to the visit in *Harzreise,* but he is equally reticent in his correspondence. Only seven months later does he allude to the encounter in a letter to his friend Christiani, and even then he gives no account of the meeting, which must have been of enormous interest to his friend. Instead, Heine contrasts, in general terms and rather grandly, his own fundamental attitude with Goethe's. Unlike Goethe, who "above all strives for a beautiful life," Heine himself, so he claims, is willing "to sacrifice his life for the idea."[7]

Heine's view of Goethe is, in fact, closely linked to his view of himself. At all times, he sees him as the epitome of the sovereign, matchless genius. He is eloquent and unstinting in his admiration for Goethe's lucidity and *Anschaulichkeit* ("concrete presentation"): "Das Wort umarmt dich, während der Gedanke dich küsst" ("The word embraces you while the thought kisses you"), he says about his poems, and he calls his prose "durchsichtig wie das grüne Meer" ("transparent as the green sea," 5:58)—praise which no doubt he would like to earn for himself. He also feels akin to Goethe in his emancipation from religious dogmatism and admires him as the "great Hellene" who joyously embraces life. On the other hand, Heine scolds him for his ivory tower detachment, all the more so since Goethe has such a potentially powerful voice in Germany. And his critique of "das grosse Weltablehnungsgenie"—the great genius in rejecting the world—is equally eloquent as is his praise. To be sure, this critique is not without implications for Heine himself. By faulting Goethe for his indifference to the currents of contemporary history, does he not, by inference, clear a niche for the one who is the torch bearer in the cause of liberation, the representative poet of his age, just as Goethe was the crowning glory of the classical period? A decade or so later, when Heine wants to defend his right as an "autonomous artist," albeit a politically aware one, he will look upon Goethe as an ally and example in opposition to Ludwig Börne. At any rate, the dialogue with Goethe, overt or not, runs like a counterpoint through Heine's entire work.

Dialectic of Progress

"Die Nordsee III" (companion piece to the two cycles of free verse) takes us on an intellectual voyage which, with its ebb and flood of reflection, seems to capture the movement of the sea. As if the expanse and freedom of the ocean inspired a similar flow of thought, the author's mind reaches out, ranging over such diverse topics as the mode of life of the island population of Norderney and the effect of tourists upon it, reflections about coins, the transmigration of souls, the Catholic church, German history, the arrogance of aristocrats, folktales, bathing beauties, Lord Byron, Sir Walter Scott, Goethe, and Napoleon—to name a few. They are all treated with lightness and humor and linked by ingenious transitions that add to the whimsical effect.

The underlying theme is the opposition of the primitive contentment of the local inhabitants and the sense of conflict and alienation which progress brings. The islanders, living in a close-knit community, are secure in their naive faith, sense of belonging, and shared interest; so secure, in fact, that they seem at times able to communicate without words. By contrast, the articulate and enlightened visitor (read, "Heine") feels "wir leben im Grunde geistig einsam" ("we actually are spiritually alone," 3:90). Heine's term for it is *Zerrissenheit* ("torn-apartness"), a condition close to the sense of alienation and existential anguish with which twentieth-century readers are all too familiar.

Unlike the rather straightforward contrast between Philistine rigor and poetic imagination which informed "Die Harzreise," the antithesis that runs through "Die Nordsee" is ambivalent and problematic. The author begins the sketch with the statement "Die Insulaner sind blutarm und leben vom Fischfang" ("the islanders are anemic and live by fishing") and goes on to mention that it is not uncommon for a father and all his sons to perish in one storm-tossed boat. These are not exactly idyllic conditions. Yet the people of Norderney seem placidly happy. Similarly, was there more happiness in the olden days, Heine wonders, when believers derived comfort and emotional security from their childlike religious trust? He gives his answer in one of the key passages of the essay: "Wir wissen [auch], dass ein Glück, das wir der Lüge verdanken, kein wahres Glück ist und dass wir, in den einzelnen zerrissenen Momenten eines gottgleicheren Zustandes, einer höheren Geisteswürde, mehr Glück empfinden können als in den lang hin-vegetierten Jahren eines dumpfen Köhlerglaubens" ("We [also] know that the happiness which we owe to a lie is no true happiness and that we are able to experience greater happiness in the rare, torn moments of a more godlike condition, of a higher, more dignified state of mind, than in all the long years of vegetating in [a] mindless belief," 3:91).

His nostalgia for the age of innocence and comforting certainties notwithstanding, Heine knows that the sense of security afforded by traditional faith is an illusion. Awed by the miracle of the human mind, he is committed to the idealist belief in enlightenment and the perfec-tability of the world through education. But the price to be paid for critical clarity, for heightened awareness—in short, for the divine gift of reason—is *Zerrissenheit* and, in the term which he coined for Byronic melancholia, *Weltschmerz* ("world-pain"). The student of Hegel realizes that a return to the age of innocence is not possible. Instead, Heine asks the question which henceforth will be paramount in his mind: how is the conflict to be reconciled, wherein lies the healing synthesis? This is the fertile ground on which Saint-Simonian ideas soon will fall.

In the meantime, a sense of superiority and elitist pride compensates for the loneliness of the critical intellectual who belongs to neither the bourgeoisie nor the aristocracy and who refuses to join the flight into Biedermeier escapism, Romantic fantasy, or religious orthodoxy. Heine views his *Zerrissenheit* as a test and proof that he is a true spokesman for his age. To experience the collective predicament of the time, he is convinced, is the curse and the blessing of the poet. When the world is out of joint, how can the poet who feels more than anyone else the heartbeat of the age, help but feel the conflicting pull within himself?

The Historic View

"Jedes Zeitalter, wenn es neue Ideen bekommt, bekommt auch neue Augen" (3:98). Each period acquires new eyes, Heine had said in "Die Nordsee": a rather remarkable insight into the relativity and changeability of human values, especially if we consider that he lived in the shadow of the classical poets, who espoused absolute norms of universal and lasting validity. In "Ideen—Das Buch LeGrand," the essay which he wrote more or less concurrently with "Nordsee," Heine presents the historic view, and shows fragments of reality as phases and stages of a world in flux. The following baroque agglomeration of unrelated items ("Iliad, Plato, battle of Marathon, Moses, Venus of Medici, Strasbourg Cathedral, the French Revolution, Hegel, steamships," 3:130) is part of a process—as is also the author's own life. He is approaching his thirtieth birthday, and like many another before and after him, he feels prompted at this juncture to look back on his own beginning: the journey which makes up this *Reisebild* leads into his childhood in Düsseldorf.

"Ideen—Das Buch LeGrand": the double-barreled title reflects the two main themes. *Ideen* ("ideas") refers to his seemingly frivolous but in fact earnestly meant reckoning with idealist attitudes. "LeGrand" was the name of a (fictitious) drummer in Napoleon's army and a devoted follower of the emperor who expresses his love of Napoleon through his drumming. Its point of departure is the unhappy lover's plight, the theme which dominates Heine's poetry but of which the prose author makes short shrift. He—the narrating "I" of the essay—had already bought his pistols. But when a gourmet meal (as well as a passing beauty) reminds him of earth's sweet attractions, he abandons the Wertherian pose, discards his pistols, and opts for life. Amusing and flippant, this episode actually sums up Heine's fundamental conviction that life is its own reward. Rather than counting on transcendental meaning and justification for his existence, man should seek fulfillment here and now. Enthusiasm for truth and freedom ("the idea") goes hand in hand with the enjoyment of lobster bisque and apple tarts. Indeed, abstract ideals are meaningful only if realized in sensual experience: freedom ultimately means freedom to live, not merely to survive. Food and reference to culinary pleasure therefore serve as a multifaceted metaphor throughout Heine's work, in terms both of basic social needs (*Die grosse Suppenfrage*, "the great soup question") and of luxuriating sensuality, the enjoyment of the fruits of this earth.

Heine calls this essay his "Dichtung and Wahrheit" ("fiction and truth"). Goethe's autobiography seems in fact to have provided a sort of matrix for Heine's memoir. Several events may be interpreted as analogies—albeit by way of contrast or inversion—of incidents in the renowned model. While Goethe tells of influences that helped form his view of a harmonious universe, Heine conjures up memories which show the dynamics of history.

For example, the naive trust of the child Goethe was shaken by news of the devastating earthquake of Lisbon. The nine-year-old Harry Heine felt similarly upset by the abdication of the Kurfürst of Palatinate-Zweibrücken, which made him realize "dass den Fürsten die Krone nicht am Kopf festgewachsen" ("that crowns were not permanently attached to the heads of princes"). The shock surfaced as a dream about the end of the world: the lovely gardens were rolled up as if they were carpets, sun and moon were taken down and put in a box, like props after the play is over. This poignantly beautiful episode contains one of Heine's earliest formulations of the statement that god is dead (3:140).

Prominent in Goethe's *Dichtung und Wahrheit* is the figure of the *Königsleutnant* ("king's lieutenant") who was billeted in the Goethe home for a time and who broadened young Wolfgang's understanding of art. Heine invents a similar military houseguest. His drummer LeGrand conveys to young Harry a feel for the movement of history, and especially, his admiration for his hero Napoleon. Modern readers may be intrigued by the author's technique in presenting Napoleon through the medium of the drum and from the perspective of the little man,[8] as one who fulfilled the goals of the French Revolution. To Heine's German contemporaries, his portrayal of the national enemy as *Geschäftsführer des Zeitgeists*—executive manager of the spirit of the time—seemed a shocking and dangerous affront. Although Napoleon was long since dead (1821), the second volume of *Reisebilder* was banned. ("Harzreise" had merely been forbidden reading in Metternich's Austria and was unobtainable in Göttingen.) After 1835, all volumes of the *Reisebilder* were on the proscribed list.

Journey to Italy

Three travel sketches resulted from Heine's Italian journey ("Reise von München nach Genua," "Die Stadt Lucca," and "Die Bäder von Lucca" [Journey from Munich to Genoa, The Town of Lucca, and The Baths of Lucca]). Whereas others had traveled south in search of Greco-Roman culture, Heine was intent on observing current sociopolitical conditions. It was, incidentally, yet another form of his "insurrection against Goethe". Goethe's Italian journey, as every German schoolchild knows, had served to crystallize his image of antiquity and consolidate his attitude of detachment. Heine traveled by the identical route—at least as far as Verona—but a more contrasting point of view is hardly imaginable. His comment is pointedly subjective and filled with trenchant criticism of existing conditions, culminating in a panegyric on "the great task of our time . . . emancipation":

Not only that of the Irish, Greeks, Frankfurt Jews, West Indian Negroes, and similarly oppressed people, but the emancipation of the whole world, especially of Europe, which has come of age and is now breaking loose from the iron leash of the privileged, the aristocracy. . . . Every age has its own challenge, and by meeting it, mankind advances. Perhaps the former inequality created by the European feudal system was necessary in order to bring about the advance of civilization. . . . The socially conscious French, more than any other people, naturally resented this inequality. . . . They tried to enforce equality by gently cutting off the heads of those who insisted on standing out, and the revolution became a signal for mankind's war of liberation. May the French be praised! They took care of the two greatest needs of human society, good food and social equality. . . . (3:259)

If liberation is the new task, its main enemy—besides aristocratic privilege and Metternich's oppressive regime which upholds it—is the religious establishment and the clergy. They form the target of "Die Stadt Lucca." But Heine draws a careful distinction between a personal sense of religiosity and institutionalized religion:

> Things used to be different in the old days. No one would have thought of especially recommending . . . his own religion, much less of forcing it on anyone. Religion meant a dear tradition, holy tales, memories, and mysteries, passed on from the ancestors. . . . A Greek would have been shocked if a stranger . . . had requested to be included in his religious rites; and he would have considered it still more barbaric to induce anyone, by coercion or ruse, to give up his native religion and accept a foreign one instead. But there came a people out of Egypt, fatherland of crocodiles and priests, bringing, along with skin diseases and stolen gold and silver vessels, a so-called positive religion, a so-called church, a framework of dogmas that must be believed, of holy ceremonials that must be carried out, a paradigm for latter-day state religions. Now began the carping abuse of humanity, the proselytizing, religious intolerance, and all those holy horrors that have cost mankind blood and tears. (3:399f.)

Note how this passage, which reveals Heine's bitterness about Christian proselytizing, relies on a contrasting frame of reference to drive home its point. The nostalgic portrayal of ancient Greek attitudes creates a foil which throws Christian practice sharply into relief.

For Heine's penetrating mind, everything becomes a metaphor. That is to say, he not only regards facts and events as manifestations of ideas but, conversely, he likes to use anecdotal episodes and fictional material to make his points. This fictionalization increasingly develops in the Italian sketches as his ideological intent deepends, his focus sharpens, and his manipulation of the material becomes ever-more deliberate and crafty.

In "Die Bäder von Lucca" [Baths of Lucca], possibly Heine's most humorous—certainly his most farcical—prose work, invented elements predominate. This sketch describes the escapades of a Jewish parvenu banker named Christopher Gumpel who converts to Catholicism and as Marquese Christophoro di Gumpelino travels to Italy to immerse himself in his newly acquired culture. The joke is that the banker's frame of reference remains firmly in place. His plain and honest companion—Sancho Pansa to this Don Quixote—is a Hamburg lottery dealer named Hyazinth Hirsch whose hilarious malapropisms (brilliant examples of the author's linguistic virtuosity) effectively expose his friend's pretentions. This parody of the parvenu and the convert—especially the convert who takes his conversion seriously—is above all a spoof on Catholic mystique and hollow aestheticism. Underlying the burlesque is the serious theme of the Jewish identity crisis and the dilemma of divided allegiance which never ceased to concern Heine deeply.

But there is more. The Italian sketches end on a rather unfortunate note, with a satire on the poet Count August von Platen-Hallermünde. It lampoons Platen's pseudoclassical formalism and mocks his homosexuality in a devastating attack which mixes clever literary satire with personal invective. The ensuing literary scandal ultimately hurt Heine as much as his victim. Actually, Platen had attacked Heine first with a crude anti-Semitic insult. Moreover, Heine suspected Platen of having intrigued against him in Munich, where his attempts to obtain the professorship were thwarted by anti-Semitic and reactionary opposition. Rightly or wrongly, Heine perceived Platen as representing the archenemy, and he was not one to turn the other cheek, precisely, perhaps, because Jews were expected to submit meekly to humiliating treatment: "If the count wants to try a little dance, let him say so; I'll play for him." This motto—a quote from Mozart's *Figaro*—precedes "Die Bäder von Lucca." Ferocious but also very funny, the Platen passages have sometimes been expunged by protective editors who considered them an aberration. But Heine's tendency to overract when provoked is as much a part of him as is his tenderness and empathy, his courage or his consciousness of human dignity.

The English at Home

A four months' sojourn in England yielded a group of short pieces which, under the title "Englische Fragmente" [English fragments], round out the *Reisebilder*. They are gems of wit and sociopolitical insight, sparked by a peculiar antagonism toward the English.

In his first encounter with parliamentary democracy, the author is shocked by the evidence of political intrigue and the clash of selfish interests. Instead of a paradise of freedom, he finds a blatantly discriminatory caste system; instead of emancipation, a narrow-minded puritanism. The legal system strikes him as downright medieval.

Visiting the Old Bailey, he is amused by the flowing wigs and gowns of the judges but not at all by their religious intolerance toward the Irish. He notes that power continues to be vested in the land which may be leased but is never sold—just as in the darkest Middle Ages. Contrasting the political idealism of the French with English pragmatism, he clearly faults the English when he observes that opposition between Whigs and Tories is not based on principle but on habit and family tradition. Moreover, since the lower classes regard aristocratic privilege as immutable and sacrosanct, and defend it more fiercely than do the lords themselves, there exists no opposition to the aristocracy. In short, Heine claims that the impressive English parlimentarianism benefits mainly the upper classes.

The areas which, in his view, are most in need of reform are the electoral system, taxation, criminal law, and religion—and, of course, English cuisine. His indictment is summed up in the anecdote about the waiter who almost fell over backward when a customer requested sugar with his cauliflower—"a heresy against the Anglican cuisine": no one since the Roman invasion has done anything to cauliflower except boil it in water (3:428).

It is surprising that Heine, who later in life abhorred any kind of ideological fanaticism and radicalism, did not appreciate English pragmatism or recognize its inherent capacity for reform. He never overcame his dislike for a people who, in his view, epitomized the cold, self-satisfied, avaricious shopkeeper and antipoetic Philistine.

In conclusion, because the *Reisebilder* are so scintillating and amusing, it is necessary to emphasize their thematic coherence and critical thrust. But it seems unfair to end on this note. Their charm derives from their ability to lift the blinkers with which familiarity tends to equip us, and thus to reengage our senses and make us aware of our surroundings. Their overriding ingredient is their humor, irony, and wit—not an irony which dissolves reality as does the so-called romantic irony but, on the contrary, an irony which destroys illusion and exposes reality. Heine's wit often illumines the landscape like a flash of lightning. His humor stimulates, engages, and provokes us but, most importantly, it makes us laugh with a laughter that blends serious concern with pleasurable release.

In a "Schlusswort", his epilogue to *Reisebilder* dated November, 1830 (that is, a few months after the July Revolution) Heine tells the story of

Kunz von der Rosen, the court jester who came to visit and cheer his emperor (Charles V) when he was imprisoned and deserted by all his knights:

"Oh, my German fatherland—dear German people—I am your Kunz von der Rosen. [Here the voice obviously blends with the author's.] The man whose proper function was entertainment and who was only supposed to amuse you in good times, he makes his way into your prison in time of need. Here under my cloak I bring to you your mighty scepter and your beautiful crown. Do you not know me, my emperor? If I cannot set you free, I will at least comfort you, and you shall have someone around to make light of your distress, to help you keep up your courage, and to love you; and whose last drop of wit and blood is at your service. . . . The day of liberation is at hand, a new age begins. My emperor, the night is over and outside glows the dawn."

"Kunz von der Rosen, my fool, you are wrong. You may have mistaken a shining hatchet for the sun, and the red glow of morning is nothing but blood."

"No, my Emperor, it is the sun, though it rises in the West. For six thousand years we have seen it rise in the East; it is time for a change."

"Kunz von der Rosen, my fool, you have lost the bells from your red cap and now it has an odd look about it, your red cap."

"Alas, my emperor, I shook my head so furiously over your distress, that the foolish bells fell off—but that did not make it a bad cap."[9] . . .

"Kunz von der Rosen, my fool, when I am free again, what will you do then?"

"I will sew new bells on my cap."

"And how shall I reward your faithfulness?"

"Oh, dear master, do not have me put to death." (3:489–92)

Chapter Four
Reports and Essays
Foreign Correspondent

Heine's arrival in Paris begins the most fruitful period of his career as reporter, political commentator, and essayist. As a correspondent for German papers—notably Cotta's distinguished *Augsburger Allgemeine Zeitung* and *Morgenblatt*—and contributor to various French journals—such as the *Revue de Paris,* the *Revue des Deux Mondes, Europe littéraire,* and the *Nouvelle Revue Germanique*—Heine proved himself to be an astute observer of the cultural and political scene. Whatever his subject matter, whether he comments on painting, music, or the theater, he never loses sight of their connection with sociopolitical realities; he views all cultural phenomena as *Signaturen,* signs and imprints of historic trends. Heine interprets day-to-day politics in terms of underlying currents and long-range effects, and his descriptions of the manipulations of the regime, in its attempt to steer a course midway between the republican left and the aristocratic right, are as colorful as they are penetrating. In time, he will sadly concede that the true victors of the July Revolution were not the poor, little people as he originally thought but the money-hungry middle-class, "a bourgeoisie which is no better than the aristocracy whose place it took" (6:140).

The reports from Paris are written in the same lucid and breezy style, with the same irony and whimsy that had intrigued and charmed the readers of *Reisebilder.* Metternich, not deceived by the light touch, saw a threat to Biedermeier contentment in these articles about French affairs, with their focus on the concerns of a constitutional monarchy. He communicated his displeasure to Baron Cotta, and Heine's position as foreign correspondent for the *Augsburger Allgemeine Zeitung* was terminated.

Heine's Paris letters subsequently appeared in book form as part of the four volumes of the *Salon.* Further commentaries, written a decade later when Heine resumed his reportage for Cotta, were gathered in the collection entitled *Lutetia* (the Roman name for Paris). French historians value Heine as the foremost witness of the reign of Louis Philippe. In Germany he acquired the reputation, for good or ill, of being a father of modern journalism.

In the first piece from Paris, a review of an exhibit of contemporary paintings in the Louvre ("Französische Maler," [French Painters], 1831), attention centers on the thematic content of the displayed works. The paintings are judged according to the way in which they express timely concerns and "the spirit of the age," that is, the idea of emancipation. Pride of place, in the critic's report, is given to the painting by Delacroix which depicts the Revolution, with the Goddess of Liberty wearing a red Jacobin cap and passionately waving the tricolor.

When, six years later, Heine writes about the French stage ("Uber die französische Bühne," 1837), he again concentrates on the sociological links, in contrast to the strictly aesthetic and dramaturgical criteria applied by traditional German critics from Gottsched to Tieck. (In this connection, he draws some intriguing comparisons between French and German sexual mores, noting that Germanic people tend to court, and celebrate in song, only unmarried maidens, whereas the French look upon the married woman as an object worthy of love, in life and in art.)

Heine's direct and explicit comments about the French political and social scene are contained in ten reports submitted to the *Augsburg Allgemeine Zeitung* during 1831/1832, and later published under the title "Französische Zustände" [The French Situation]. Here, the author's euphoria about the rosy new dawn gives way to a realistic assessment of French day-to-day politics and politicking. Optimistic generalizations about the new order are replaced by shrewd appraisals of the various factions that compete for power, and by thoughtful reflections on the intellectual influences that have shaped the attitudes of the antagonists, specifically, of the different "men of the Revolution." It is noteworthy that Heine rarely refers to the economic causes of the French Revolution but believes, above all, in the power of ideas.

Of special interest are his views on communism that are gradually beginning to form. Looking back on 1789, he characterizes the opposition of Robespierre and Danton as a manifestation of a basic dualism, originally introduced and represented by Rousseau and Voltaire, of a radical, ascetic rigorism and a more relaxed, easygoing attitude toward revolution.[1] Needless to say, he himself tends to sympathize and identify with Voltaire's *legèreté* rather than with Rousseau's cultural pessimism.

In the days of the July monarchy, this controversy was to acquire new currency with the revival of the influence of Gracchus Babeuf, one of the early utopian socialists who was executed in the aftermath of the French Revolution. Babeuf's ideas were newly circulated[2] and formed the basis of the growing republican opposition to Louis Philippe's regime. Babeuf and his followers—who in 1834 began to gather in secret societies—advocated complete equality. They demanded not merely equality before the law but *juissances communes,* "equality in the enjoyment of the fruit of this earth," in Heine's terms. Babeuf, like his spiritual mentor Rousseau, looked on the arts and on culture as superfluous frills.

For Heine this poses a real dilemma which, in the course of his career, will cause him to make seemingly contradictory statements, alternately welcoming revolution as a just, and indeed inevitable, solution to human problems, and expressing his fear about the cultural wasteland which it will bring about. If seen in context, his pronouncements are not as inconsistent as they appear to be when juxtaposed indiscriminately. However, he becomes increasingly aware that no simplistic solution is possible and rarely hides his profound sense of ambivalence. He sounds least worried (and most radical) during the period of his close association with Karl Marx (1844).[3] Marx, who neither denounced culture himself nor dismissed art as irrelevant, seems to have allayed Heine's fear, at least temporarily. It is, in fact, likely that Marx not only reassured Heine but that his own appreciation of the importance of art and artists may, in turn, have been stimulated by the poet Heine, whom he greatly admired and frequently quoted. The one and only passage in his oeuvre where Marx expresses fear of "crude communism" is contained in the third of the so-called Paris manuscripts, written at the time of his friendship with Heine.[4]

Heine's concern about the bleak prospect for the arts in an egalitarian society resurfaced and intensified later on, especially after the tumultuous riots of 1848, some of which he witnessed at close range when the chaise which was to take him to the hospital was overturned. His gloomy prediction is most vividly articulated in a passage from the French preface to *Lutetia* from the year 1855:

Anxiety and terror fill me when I think of the time when these iconoclasts will come to power. Their heavy hands will ruthlessly shatter the marble effigies of beauty so dear to my heart. They will put an end to the whimsical play things of art which the poet cherishes. They will plow up the laurel groves and plant potatoes. They will root out from the soil of society the lilies that neither toil nor spin. . . . The nightingales, those unnecessary songsters, will be chased away and alas, my *Book of Songs* will serve as bags in which the grocer of the future will wrap coffee or snuff for old women. . . . Yet this communism, so threatening to my peace of mind, so opposed to my interests, casts a spell over me. . . . I cannot struggle against its logic. If I admit the syllogism that "every man has a right to eat," than I must agree not only to the premise but to all its implications and consequences. . . . The old social order has long since been judged and condemned. . . . May it perish, the old society where the innocent went under, where selfishness thrived, and man was exploited by man. . . . Let the old order be destroyed. . . . Hail, then, to the grocer who shall take my poems and make them into bags for the old women's snuff and coffee, comforts which, too often in this unjust world, are denied them. Fiat justitia, pereat mundus! (6:247)

Spiritualism and Sensualism

While attempting to inform German readers about the lively goings-on in contemporary France, Heine also sought to acquaint the French with German thinking. Prompted by Madame de Staël's *De l'Allemagne* which, in his opinion, presented an idealized view of Germany and especially of the Romantic Movement, he undertook to give his version of the story. It first appeared in French, with a dedication to Prosper Enfantin.

But the twin essays, in their final German form entitled *Die Geschichte der Religion und Philosophie in Deutschland* [History of Religion and Philosophy in Germany] and *Die Romantische Schule* [The Romantic School], contain a reinterpretation and revaluation of intellectual history that is no less revelatory for the German reader. They constitute a unique achievement: It is difficult to recall another instance where such a complicated and esoteric content as the evolution of German metaphysical thought is conveyed in a similarly colorful, lively manner. These essays—together with *Ludwig Börne* which followed in 1837—give the most coherent account of Heine's views in his middle period. Here his personal experience and inclination, merging with Hegelian as well as Saint-Simonian ideas and expressed in his special style, have resulted in an original work which in turn has influenced other thinkers from Marx to Nietzsche, Freud, and Jung.

Heine's main concern is the liberation from the triple yoke of religious, sociopolitical, and sexual bondage. He postulates a synthesis which would do away with the opposing pull of spiritualism and sensualism that was introduced by Judeo-Christian tradition. In effect, he redefines Western society's moral values. Going back to the source of the dichotomy, to biblical, Gnostic, and Manichean, and still more ancient Persian concepts, he explains the

essence of the Christian idea [as] the doctrine of two principles. . . .; an evil Satan forever stands in opposition to the good Christ: the world of spirit is represented by Christ, the material world by Satan. Our soul belongs to the former, our body to the latter. The whole physical world—Nature—is therefore fundamentally evil and Satan, the prince of darkness, wants to lure us through it to destruction. It behooves us therefore to renounce all sensual pleasures, to punish our bodies, Satan's fief, so that our soul may soar all the more gloriously upward into the light of heaven. . . . This fundamental Christian world view spread with incredible speed over the whole Roman empire, like an infectious disease that lasted throughout the Middle Ages. (5:179f.)

Heine notes the negative impact of this belief on all aspects of life: the debilitating psychological effect of asceticism and sensual deprivation, the social consequences of a devaluation of material and secular concerns, and the political servitude resulting from the exploitation of these beliefs. For he sees a pernicious alliance between political overlords and the clergy, each relying on the other to help maintain their dominion. But for all his attacks on the political and ecclesiastic establishment, his critique is mainly aimed at the underlying concepts and tenets. What makes his views so radical is not that he criticizes the church or the hypocrisy of its adherents—others had done that before him—but that he questions the very basis of Christian morality.

One day when humanity regains its health, when peace is restored between body and spirit and they merge again in their original harmony, we will scarcely be able to comprehend the unnatural discord that Christianity has sewn. Happier and more beautiful generations, begotten in a union of free choice and flourishing in a religion of joy, will smile sadly at their poor ancestors who gloomily abstained from all the pleasure of this beautiful earth. . . . Yes, I believe in progress, I believe that mankind is destined to be happy, and thus I have a higher opinion of the deity than those pious souls who imagine that God created man only to suffer. It is here on earth that I should like to see established, through social and political institutions, that blissful existence which, according to the pious, is to await us only on the Day of Judgment, in heaven. (5:180)

In a bold line, he traces the development of European thought, from prebiblical times onward, as a movement of progressive secularization. Thinkers are appraised according to the role they played in this process of liberation from religious doctrine. Although presenting an over-simplified and somewhat idiosyncratic account of Western intellectual history, the essay abounds in brilliant insights and fascinating formulations. Martin Luther, Gotthold Ephraim Lessing, and Immanual Kant are seen as the three outstanding emancipators. By ridding theology from the shackles of scholasticism and inviting independent reading of the Bible, Luther prepared the way for freedom of thought; Lessing continued the education to enlightened rationalism; while Kant, "executioner of Jehovah," is perceived as having completed the intellectual revolution from which, Heine is convinced, sociopolitical liberation is sure to follow.

God is Dead

Many European thinkers have played a part in questioning and undermining the dogmatic basis of Christianity, but the message of the "death of God," with its intrinsic contradiction, is usually attributed to Nietzsche. The image of the dying God is, in fact, already fully developed in Heine's work. But whereas Nietzsche's paradoxical announcement sounds strident and harsh and obviously intends to shock, we hear from Heine an almost nostalgic lament. He is not concerned with theological or ontological speculation but only with the effect which Christian religion has had on the individual and on society. He recognizes God as a fictitious figure, yet a real and powerful force nevertheless. God's reality and power, derived from man's belief in him, is manifest and effective through the cultural and political systems which are based on this belief and, in turn, perpetuate it. As this belief dies, God dies—thus allowing social and political institutions to be changed. There is nothing paradoxical and much that is genuinely moving in the account of Jehovah's impending demise which precedes the chapter on Kant:

Of this catastrophe, Deism's January 21,[5] we shall speak in the following section. A strange awe, a mysterious piety, prevents us from writing more today. Our heart is filled with a terrible pity—it is old Jehovah himself who is preparing for death. We have known him so well, from his cradle in Egypt, where he was reared among divine calves and crocodiles, sacred onions, ibisses, and cats. We saw him as he bade farewell to these playmates of his childhood and to the obelisks and sphinxes of his native Nile valley and became a little god-king in Palestine among a poor shepherd tribe and lived in his own temple-palace. We saw him later on, when he came in contact with Assyrian-Babylonian civilization, give up his all-too-human passions, no longer spewing nothing but wrath and vengeance, at least no longer thundering at every trifle. We saw him emigrate to Rome, the capital, where he renounced all national prejudices and proclaimed the divine equality of all nations and made opposition against old Jupiter with fine phrases, and intrigued until he gained supreme power and from the Capitol ruled the city and the world, *urbem et orbem*. We saw how he became even more spiritual, how he whimpered softly and blissfully, turning into a loving father, a universal friend of man, a do-gooder, a philanthropist—but all this availed him nothing. Do you hear the little bell ringing? Kneel down. They are bringing the sacraments to a dying God. (5:256)

This passage works on several levels. Ostensibly telling the life-story of Jehovah, it does, in fact, transpose the history of monotheism into a series of tableaux, each of which illustrates a trend in Judeo-Christian development. By its placement within the total work, it assumes a structural function (not unlike the retarding moment before catastrophe strikes in classical tragedy) and underscores Kant's role as God's executioner. Nor is his "Pietät"—the reverent awe which makes Heine pause—altogether affected. While he intellectually welcomes the era of advancing rationality and its promise of sociopolitical improvement, emotionally he yearns for the age of myths, and he strongly feels the spell of the Bible.

Furthermore, throughout his life, in his formal writing and in letters, Heine refers to God as an ever-present "Du," witness, judge, and partner, or what the ancients called their muse. Such references are apt to occur even in statements which contain a rejection of conventional religion. When he warns us not to trust death-bed conversions (à propos Schelling's espousal of Catholicism), he says "Such tales of conversion . . . merely prove that it was not possible to convert those freethinkers as long as they were walking about with healthy senses under God's open heavens and were in complete possession of their reasoning faculty" (5:301). If it is a figure of speech, it is a deliberate one; double-tongued perhaps, but not a mere slip of the tongue. Clearly Heine wishes to underscore that his rejection of religious dogma goes hand in hand with an affirmation of "natural," authentic religiosity, awe for the miracle of the universe and that higher force of which human reason is a reflection ("jene erhabene Geisteskraft, die wir Vernunft nennen," "that sublime power of mind which we call reason"). He speaks of love as a divine value and calls beauty "die köperliche Offenbarung Gottes" ("God's physical manifestation"). Last but not least, he personally feels his creativity to be part, and proof, of something divine.

The main theme of *Religion und Philosophie* is the discovery of the *Schulgeheimnis* ("academic secret") of idealist philosophy, namely, the revelation that pantheism is the secret religion of Germany. The essay closes with a famous warning to the French where Heine prophetically envisions the revolutionary fury with which this pantheism will one day be unleashed. It is an oft-quoted prophecy, sometimes regarded as an anticipation of events which happened a hundred years later. With uncanny insight, Heine points to the "German problem": a nation of *Dichter und Denker* ("poets and thinkers") capable of the worst atrocities. He not only links idealism and extreme fanaticism but shows the one to be the basis of the other:

Don't smile at my advice, the advice of a dreamer, who warns you against Kantians, Fichteans, and philosophers of nature. Don't smile at the visionary who expects in the realm of reality the same revolution that has taken place in the domain of thought. The thought precedes the deed as lightning precedes thunder. German thunder, however, is truly German. Not very nimble, it comes rolling along rather slowly. But come it will, and when once you hear a crash the like of which has never before been heard in world history, then take heed: the German thunder has at last arrived. . . . A drama will be enacted in Germany compared with which the French Revolution might seem an innocent idyll. . . . And the hour will come. As on the steps of an amphitheater, the nations will group themselves around Germany to behold the great contest. . . ." (5:307f.)

End of the Age of Art

The literary aspects of the Christian-spiritualist legacy are dealt with in *Romantische Schule*. To begin with, Heine repeats his relativist (Hegelian) position with regard to the changing worth of ideas and values, depending on historic circumstances. While Christianity initially had a wholesome impact in countering the crass materialism that engulfed the Roman Empire and "threatened to destroy all the cultural grandeur of mankind," and while its "spiritualizing" influence on the "superhealthy," "all-too-full-blooded" peoples of the North marked the beginning of European civilization (5:16), its time, he contends, is now over. And inasmuch as he single-mindedly defines Romanticism as "nothing other than the revival of the poesy of the Middle Ages," a poesy which had "proceeded from Christianity, a passion-flower sprung from the blood of Christ" (5:15), he implies that Romanticism, along with Christian orthodoxy, is now obsolete and must give way to a literature that is committed to political involvement.

Heine's beloved model on the road to such literary engagement is Lessing. "Literary history is the great morgue where everyone looks for the dead whom he loves or to whom he is related" (5:26). Clearly, Heine regards Lessing as his kin. He appreciates Lessing's versatility, integrity, courage, and wit, his sensibility and critical acumen, and above all, "his works are animated by that great social idea, that progressive humanism, that religion of reason whose John the Baptist he was and whose Messiah we are still awaiting" (5:25).

Once more attention centers on Goethe, who died in 1832 (a year after Hegel) and whose death did indeed mark the end of an era. In his oft-quoted judgment on the *Kunstperiode* ("age of art") Heine draws up a final balance sheet, combining superlative praise with qualified recognition and cutting indictment. He respects the serene "Olympian" as an exponent of the pantheist world view and extolls his beautiful, "magical" language in an eloquent passage that does credit to them both (5:58). But, "Goethe's masterpieces . . . adorn our dear fatherland as beautiful statues adorn a garden, but they are, after all, statues.

You can fall in love with them, but they are sterile. . . . A deed is the child of the word, and Goethe's beautiful words are childless" (5:50). Despite his biased and rigid view of Romanticism that focuses on its retreat into medievalism and orthodoxy and on its alliance with reactionary politics, Heine draws distinctive and diverse profiles of individual Romantic authors. He appreciates Jean Paul, E. T. A. Hoffmann, Adelbert von Chamisso, and Ludwig Uhland but is critical of Tieck, Novalis, and the Schlegels.

There is nothing systematic and much that is idiosyncratic in this assembly of pen sketches, each of which seems memorable in a different way as Heine varies his method of presentation to convey the quintessential quality of each subject. For example, Hoffmann and Novalis are introduced through a description of their respective devotees. The robust, jolly, pink-cheeked postmistress is a Hoffmann fan who sends to the lending library for copies of her favorite author's works while Novalis's pretty young "muse," a moribund consumptive with serious blue eyes, is engrossed in her very own morocco-and-gold volume of *Heinrich von Ofterdingen*. And it is no coincidence that Heine claims to have last encountered the foppish figure of A. W. Schlegel, of all places, beneath Molière's window. For his wounding ridicule of his former teacher Heine has been much criticized. Without wishing to defend the tactless—though once again, hilarious—manner of his attack, it is well to remember that in this instance his motives were not personal. He assailed in Schlegel a significant and powerful influence that had been responsible for shaping Madame de Staël's view of Germany.

Heine's technique of manipulating the reader's perspective should not be emulated as a way of writing literary history. Still, *Die Romantische Schule* offers a fascinating mosaic of colorful portraits and contains many perceptive observations of interest to the modern reader. And while his treatment of Romanticism may seem anything but evenhanded—he takes no note of its essentially modern traits or of its intensified awareness of self—there can be no doubt that he foresaw, with uncanny accuracy, its long-range effect as a wellspring of German nationalism and introverted obscurantism.

Demonization

As an offshoot of *Romantische Schule*, Heine compiled a charming potpourri of myths and legends, fairy-tales and fables of Germanic and

Celtic origin. He continued to feel a special affection for German traditional tales and figures, just as he was always thinking lovingly— and the more so the longer he lived abroad—of the anonymous, unawakened Germany, the "good" Germany, the sleeping giant whose nose he liked to tweak. But even in the innocuous collection entitled "Elementargeister" [Elemental Spirits], the author introduces a serious leitmotiv, a pervasive theme, in line with his general views, by demonstrating how the Christian rejection of nature and sensuality adversely affected the happy pagan sprites and fairies: they were demonized, turned into vicious goblins, and driven underground.

One of the best-known tales contained in "Elementargeister" is the legend of Tannhäuser familiar through Wagner's opera. Wagner took over his basic theme from Heine, who concocts a highly original formulation and modification of the ancient legend. After citing the traditional version from *Des Knaben Wunderhorn,* he adds his own ironic variation, in verse. His captive in the Venusberg (Mount Venus) is not so much plagued by moral-religious scruples as he is troubled by a surfeit of pleasure and "sweet comfort." Yet even the pope cannot free him from this kind of bondage, and so Tannhäuser returns to domesticity. Like a husband after a prolonged business trip, he parries—or forestalls—uncomfortable queries by falling into a breathless recital of his alleged itinerary. It is a travelogue with a difference, however, bristling with barbed sallies at assorted political and literary targets (5:361ff.).

This poetic insert forms an interesting transition in several respects. The theme combines medieval-Christian with classical elements (the troubadour held prisoner by Venus), to which Heine adds a foray into the contemporary scene. Beginning with the closed form and archaic mode of folksong and legend, it lapses at the point of Tannhäuser's return into the casual, all-inclusive format of a versified travelogue such as Heine was to develop successfully in his mock epics. It rings a new change on the love theme, for unhappiness now results not from rejection but from too much compliance. And it is filled with ironic, self-parodying allusions to the poet's changed personal situation. He has been captured by his own Venus in the person of Crescence Eugénie Mirat (Mathilde).

Mythology, whether Teutonic, biblical, or classical, never ceases to fascinate Heine, and he achieves some of his most memorable effects by summoning mythological personages whom readers know from an altogether different context, to exemplify this or that very ordinary aspect of human behavior. (Who but Heine would think of dealing with the Proserpina myth by identifying Ceres as Pluto's mother-in-law?)

This penchant for exploiting the venerable archetypal figures for his own purposes—with at times hilarious results—finds expression in a companion piece to "Elementargeister," written some fifteen years later. "Die Götter im Exil" [Gods in Exile, 1853] describes the transformation and demonization of the gay Hellenic and Roman deities in the Christian era. Its most remarkable chapter graphically depicts a Bacchanalian orgy. What makes the episode all the more impressive is the "frame" which the author provides for it, the vantage point from which he presents it. He allows an innocent bystander, a pious, simple fisherman, to witness the shocking scene. Dumbfounded and frightened, the lad rushes the next morning to the near-by monastery to confess what he has seen—only to recognize in the father confessor one of the ribald participants in the event (7:63f.).

Poet or Activist?

In correspondence with his publisher, Heine commended his *Denkschrift für Ludwig Börne* [Memorial for Ludwig Börne] as a "precious little book" which, he felt certain, would be recognized as his best ever.[6] While such statements need to be taken with a grain of salt—Heine was, after all, negotiating the honorarium—there is reason to believe that he was in earnest about the valuation he placed on this piece. He sensed that he had revealed more of himself in this work than perhaps in any other, and really expected that its worth, if only as a superbly written and entertaining documentary of the period, would be appreciated by the readers.

In this expectation he could hardly have been more mistaken, at least as far as his contemporaries were concerned. The Börne book aroused a storm of indignation that surpassed even the furor of the Platen affair. Friends and foes alike turned on him and from him in disgust. They regarded the book as yet another attack on a colleague, like the sorties on Platen, Schlegel, and Menzel,[7] only this one was more despicable, directed as it was against a kindred spirit, a fellow liberal, and, worst of all, one unable to rejoinder (Börne had died in 1837). *Ihr Werk missfällt total* ("Your work is totally disliked"), was Laube's verdict,[8] and Campe called it Heine's "Russian campaign." In a sense Campe had contributed to the public's negative perception of the book by entitling it, against Heine's express wish, *Heine über Börne*, which may mean Heine "about" or "above" Börne; the manner in which the title page was set up suggested the latter. Heine had proposed "Ludwig Börne: Eine Denkschrift."

The notion that the Börne book was but a malicious polemic, prompted by petty motives, had a devastating effect on Heine's life and, echoed by his biographers for almost a century, it continued to plague his reputation long after his death. In recent years, some readers have expressed entirely different views. One of the first, and certainly the most prominent, among these voices was that of Thomas Mann:

> Of [Heine's] works I have long since loved his *Börne* best. Nowhere did he achieve greater heights as a writer and a world psychologist, nowhere was he more in advance of his time. . . . His psychology of the Nazarene-type anticipates Nietzsche, with his profound insight into the opposition of spirit and art (not merely morality and art), and in asking himself whether the synthesis of spiritualism and Hellenism does not perhaps represent the aim of the entire European civilization, he anticipates Ibsen and more than him. Besides, this book contains the most brilliant German prose before Nietzsche.[9]

Aberration or masterpiece? How is it possible that a work can call forth such discrepant judgments? In part the difference confirms what Heine had said about each period acquiring "new eyes." But the real cause lies elsewhere. The condemnation of the Börne book had in fact been based mainly on two offensive pages concerning Börne's ménage à trois with Jeanette Wohl and Salomon Strauss (6:177–79), and few people bothered to read the whole work. (This lacuna seems symptomatic of Heine's past reception in general: famous or infamous—yet virtually unread except for the songs and a few samples of his prose.) Only since the revival of Heine interest in the past three decades or so has *Ludwig Börne* received a close and sympathetic reading. To modern eyes, it seems fairly obvious that, whatever internal and external stimuli had prompted Heine to undertake the project in the first place—jealousy and revenge may well have played a major part—once he became engrossed in the work, its scope deepened and expanded. It contains Heine's reckoning not only with a contemporary but most of all with himself. Here he sorts out where he stands in regard to the various dilemmas which had been vexing him.[10]

He who had been so definite in declaring that the "cult of art" was obsolete, and so outspoken in his call for a more timely, activist literature, now sees the need to protect art from the opposite extreme: deterioration of form and loss of artistic integrity. His reflections on the ideal mission of the artist had recently found expression in his critical introductions to Shakespeare and Cervantes,[11] both of whom he admires as supreme masters in their respective genres because they are able to combine a sense for epochal issues with artistic excellence. To be endowed with extraordinary sensitivity and an intuitive grasp of the important issues of the age is the mark of the true artist, Heine maintains; but empathy and enthusiasm for a cause is not enough: only a sovereign, deliberate process of shaping (*Bildnerruhe*) ensures an enduring work of art.

Closely related to the conflicting pulls of political commitment and poetic detachment was another quandary. Although he unceasingly needled the Germans for their political backwardness and apathy—the recurring image is that of the German *Michel* who has his nightcap pulled deep over his eyes (based on *Schlafmütze,* which denotes both the cap and the sleeper)—Heine himself was unwilling to join any group or party. Specifically, he kept aloof from the community of German political exiles, mostly artisans, who had gathered in Paris, with Börne as the leading spirit. For all his sympathy for the aspirations of the *Volk,* the people, Heine shunned close contacts with them and had an abiding distaste for his tobacco-smoking, beer-drinking compatriots. His conviction that everyone has a right to the good life did not diminish his fear of the leveling influences to which an egalitarian society would be subjected, and he dreaded the specter of grey uniformity that would reduce all to a common mediocrity. As a consequence, he was accused of being a renegade and backslider from the liberal cause. Feared and censored as a radical, denounced as a reactionary, Heine found himself under attack—or at least under suspicion—on both fronts.

In yet another sphere did his position need clarification. His idea of emancipation was all-inclusive, inseparably linking religious, sexual, and politico-economic liberation. But in practice he observed a different alignment of forces in the alliance of republican ideology with a spiritualistic-ascetic posture. Robespierre, he notes, was a fanatical defender of old-fashioned virtue and asceticism, and so is Ludwig Börne. Börne had openly and vociferously denounced Heine's hedonism and had branded him as a libertine. Heine in turn taunted him by flaunting his sensualist preferences.

Yet in the eyes of the world, the two men seemed like brothers under the skin. Only eleven years apart—Börne is the elder—they both were regarded as members of "Young Germany," both were Jews who accepted baptism for professional reasons. Both grew up in the Rhineland where they experienced European history as affecting their lives and careers; both wrote of their time and were to be credited with being the first practitioners of feuilletonistic journalism. They were both known for their wit, displaying a similar attitude toward Germany as rebels and patriots, a combination which in their day was unique (and has only fairly recently become respectable in Germany). Above all, they were seen as exponents of liberalism. After the 1830 Revolution they emigrated to Paris. Both thought of themselves as mediators between Germany and France.

The attempt to show this resemblance to be deceptive constitutes the express theme of Heine's *Denkschrift*. Irked by the fact that their names tended to be lumped together, Heine had what must have seemed a brilliant idea at the time: to use this supposed double as a foil to establish the essential differences in their attitudes and views. He was going to draw a portrait of Börne, strictly on the basis of their personal contacts (including written ones), stressing in each instance his— Heine's—subjective perception and reaction.

Two outstanding features characterize Heine's style: he likes to present abstract thought through concrete examples and to exploit contrast and antithesis. Here he has a vehicle for both. The figure of Ludwig Börne serves, as it were, as a giant metaphor. And against the matrix of (supposed) similarity, the contrasts and differences will emerge all the more clearly. The stratagem will serve to make visible the gulf between them but also the subtle distinctions and qualifications that are less obvious. It will provide an opportunity for the author to explore, elaborate, and elucidate his own lone position amid the conflicting pulls and pressures as he proceeds to touch on just about every important topic that has ever occupied him.

Early in the book Heine establishes a fundamental difference between Börne and himself from which everything else will seem to flow. Translating the spiritual-sensual dichotomy into psychological terms, as one of contrasting temperaments, he describes the "Nazarene" (Judeo-Christian) and "Hellene" alternatives as "people given to an ascetic, abstract, anti-aesthetic [*kunstfeindlich*] intellectualizing, and those realistic and joyously expansive people who love life" respectively (6:94). He characterizes Börne as a prototype of the Nazarene disposition while presenting himself as a Hellene. (Whether Heine was in fact as "liberated" as he liked to appear, is another question.)

The book is divided into five parts. The opening chapter deals with their encounters in Germany, notably the occasion when Heine (on his way to Munich) visits Börne in Frankfurt. Walking about the Frankfurt ghetto (more precisely, the site of the former ghetto), they observe, reflect, and converse. Seemingly a casual ramble, this miniature "Reisebild" abounds with amusing anecdotes, clever reflections, and witticisms, all the while subtly introducing the differentiated response(s) of the two men. While the narrative and the conversation flow with unforced ease, linked—or so at least it seems—only by random association, crucial and pivotal topics are in fact touched upon, from Goethe and Napoleon to Judaism and the role of the Rothschilds.

The second chapter—in which Börne's name is not mentioned—consists of the famous "Letters from Helgoland." The author claims to be quoting from diaries that originated immediately before and after the 1830 Revolution. Beautifully written, these "Letters" admirably capture the sense of expectation and enthusiasm of the period and convey Heine's basic view of the revolution as a culmination of the emancipatory process. It is here that the important link between life-affirming sensuality, progressive humanism, and sociopolitical liberation is established. Like other "sons of the Enlightenment," Heine believes in the continuum of intellectual history, in a meaningful evolution toward something. This goal which for Herder was *Humanität* ("humanitas") Heine calls revolution, meaning liberation of man's full human potential. Those who call Heine a mere "hedonist" tend to overlook that he stresses sensual needs mainly because they have been suppressed: his ideal is a synthesis of the physical and the spiritual.

As one example of a harmonious union of spirit and matter he cites the Old Testament, in a truly brilliant, beautiful panegyric: "What a

book! Big and wide as the world, rooted deep in the abyss of creation
and reaching upward into the blue mysteries of heaven. Sunrise and
sunset, promise and fulfillment, birth and death, the whole drama of
mankind, it is all contained in this book. . . . It is the book of books,
Biblia" (6:118). But the author's special praise is reserved for its
language:

"Even more remarkable than the content to me is its manner, with the word
just as much a natural product as is a tree, a flower, the sea, the stars, man
himself. It seems to flow, to sparkle, to smile, to grow, one does not know
how, one does not know why, it all seems perfectly natural. . . . Its style is
that of a notebook in which the absolute spirit . . . enters the events of the
day with about the same matter-of-factness with which we make out our
laundry lists." (6:125)

The one author of modern times whose style, with its combination of
earthiness and spirituality, at times approaches biblical immediacy, is
William Shakespeare:

In Shakespeare, too, the word sometimes emerges in an awesome nakedness
which shocks and moves us. In his works we sometimes meet truth incarnate
without the garment of artifice. . . . Shakespeare is at once Jew and Greek;
or rather, spirituality and art have harmoniously combined within him to
form a greater whole. Is this kind of harmonious synthesis of the two
elements perhaps the ultimate goal of all European civilization? (6:126)

With this question, Heine returns to the basic theme of the "Letters
from Helgoland"; or rather, he reminds us that he has not really
deviated from it.

Considerable controversy among scholars has centered on the genesis
of the "Letters,"[12] but the consensus now seems to be that Heine really
used some original manuscripts, composed probably a few months after
July, 1830, but that in their deliberately crafted final form they were
produced much later, in conjunction with the Börne book. In any
event, they achieve the desired effect of recapturing the mood of
optimistic anticipation.

The radiant central image for this *Enthusiasmusperiode* ("period of
enthusiasm") is *Juliussonne* ("the July sun"). The metaphor itself seems
to act like a firework, erupting into a burst of secondary explosions.
This is a good example of Heine's use of image and of his special talent

for expanding and enriching a metaphor by uncovering additional points of comparison in the periphery of the central meaning. In this instance, the main metaphor, which recurs throughout his work, is that of the sun as the symbol for light, enlightenment, clarity, reason, and progress. (The moon, by contrast, represents romanticism and dark mystery, while the stars stand for ideals and absolutes.) "Julius" Sonne: the archaic form already provides a certain flavor by alluding to the mighty emperor after whom the month is named. The idea that the revolution of July, 1830, was somehow the result of *die Juliussonne* is conveyed by the way in which the arrival of the news—truly a news flash, albeit a week late—is announced: "das dicke Zeitungspaket, mit den warmen, glühend heissen Neuigkeiten. . . . Es waren Sonnenstrahlen, eingewickelt in Druckpapier, und sie entflammten meine Seele . . ." ("The thick bundle of newspapers arrived with its glowing, red-hot news. They were rays of sunshine wrapped in newsprint, and they set my soul ablaze," 6:130). Three pages later, further facets of the motif are revealed when the author comments that one of those wild, paper-wrapped sunbeams must have touched his very brain: "No water will quench this Greek fire." He then goes on to describe how the "Parisian sunstroke" affected the other tourists as well, each in a different way (6:133). Thus compiled, these references—the list could be continued—seem like a baroque exercise in rhetoric; coming upon them in context, the reader actually savors these fresh and startling links with the core image while becoming increasingly aware of the unfolding relevancy and satisfying aptness of the analogy. It even spills over into the next chapter which deals with the reunion of the two men in Paris. When he visits him there for the first time, Heine is struck by Börne's emaciated appearance. What little flesh Börne had, is gone— "possibly melted by the rays of the *Juliussonne*" (6:141). Thus, by metaphoric innuendo, the function of these inserted "Letters" is underscored anew. They were to establish the emotional and ideological basis of Heine's revolutionary idealism, but also to prepare for the rift between Börne and himself.

This rift emerges as the author begins to delineate the parting of their ways, implying that while he himself kept his broadly based vision of universal emancipation intact, Börne was turning into a fanatical, blinkered ideologue and political activist. With deft and amusing strokes—accomplishing with words what latter-day cartoonists would express with drawings—Heine proceeds to caricature the German would-be revolutionaries assembled in Paris, with Börne presiding over them but actually controlled by them. Yet although Heine pokes fun at the assorted members of this "menagerie," the reader cannot help sensing his affection and sympathy for their aspirations. His caustic derision and scorn is reserved for the people on whom he focuses in the next segment, those whom he unflinchingly brands as the real enemies: the German nationalists or, as he calls them, *Teutomanen* ("Teutomaniacs"). Once again, his words have a prophetic ring: "Narrow-minded Teutomania . . . that blubbered about love and faith, but its love was nothing but hatred of all things foreign, and its faith nothing but blind unreason. In its ignorance, it inspired nothing better than the burning of books" (6:171). He goes on to point to the thoroughness with which some of his "Olde-German friends" in a Göttingen Bierkeller prepared proscription lists for the day when they would come to power: "Anyone descended from a Frenchman, Jew, or Slav, even in the seventh generation, was condemned to exile" (6:171). (Worse than exile even Heine could not foresee!)

The concluding chapter begins with an interesting reversal which allows Börne's voice to be heard, by quoting at length Börne's critique of Heine's "Französische Zustände" (1833). In this highly critical review, Börne accused Heine of inconsistency, frivolousness, and lack of character, and he faulted Heine for placing art above the cause of freedom. Most of these accusations Heine has (or believes he has) already refuted in the course of the book, or rather, inverted and turned into compliments, with implied criticism of the accuser (for instance, his own more profound understanding of liberation in contrast to Börne's fanatical limitation; or his Hellenist openness in contrast to Börne's Nazarene hypocrisy). Now the attention turns to the polarity of "character" and "talent." By his very definition of character, Heine manages to turn the alleged fault into an asset:

What is understood by the word character? A person whose behavior is determined by a definite view of life and who identifies with it without internal conflict is said to have character. In the case of outstanding minds who tower above their age, the multitude can never know whether they have character or not, because it does not possess a wide enough horizon to take in the circles within which those superior minds move. Ignorant of the scope of their aspirations . . . it may happen that the masses see neither moral authority nor necessity in their actions, and the myopic and stupid crowd complains about arbitrariness, inconsistency, and lack of character. Less gifted men whose more superficial and narrower view of life is more readily grasped, have, as it were, proclaimed their life's program in the marketplace, in popular language, and once and for all. The upright public can always understand these men, it has a yardstick for their every action and it is pleased with its own intelligence, just as one is at guessing a charade. It shouts happily: "Look, this is a man of character!" (6:215)

As for "talent"—the main intent of the Börne book seems to have been to differentiate between the well-intentioned, honest, upright citizen who also happens to be a writer, and the "autonomous artist," the true poet who by (Heine's) definition is the mouthpiece of his age by virtue of his heightened sensitivity and special genius, an extraordinary person who cannot be measured by standards of the common crowd. It is not an easy distinction to maintain and rather a matter of emphasis. For Heine it was a vexing question that he could not really resolve. Nor have others been able to draw a clear line. The theme is a hardy perennial in German literature, from Goethe to Thomas Mann and Günter Grass.

The Börne book is studded with interesting and amusing utterances. Some of these show remarkable insight into the workings of the human mind. Suspecting that feeling is the true determinant, even where reason seems to be in charge; and sensing the secret power of repressed or unconscious emotions, Heine anticipated the concepts of rationalization, sublimation, and *ressentiment* which were to be developed by Nietzsche and Freud (e.g., 6:93, 97). Poignant and profoundly moving comments convey the pain of exile and the particular misery of the poet whose very thoughts are "exiled in a foreign language" (6:208).

The "portrait" of Börne which the book purports to draw is, needless to say, stereotyped, some astute and accurate observations notwithstanding; just as Heine's view of intellectual history, despite its brilliantly revealing vistas, is a product of biased generalization. The fact that *Ludwig Börne* is a mixture of documentary, fiction, autobiography, polemic, and essay which defies generic categorization, has probably played a part in its neglect. It need not deter modern readers.

Chapter Five

Experiments in Fiction

The German edition of *Geschichte der Religion und Philosophie* had been mutilated by the censor to such a degree that Heine feared that what he termed his basic "patriotic-democratic" intention had been completely lost (5:168). But matters were to worsen. If he, convinced that the thought begets the deed, believed in the practical consequences of ideas, so did Prince Metternich. In December, 1835, the Federal German Assembly (prompted by Metternich) issued a decree which banned the writings of the so-called Jungdeutsche, the Young Germans, specifically naming Ludwig Wienbarg, Theodor Mundt, Heinrich Laube, Karl Gutzkow, and Heinrich Heine, whom Metternich regarded as the leader of a dangerous conspiracy. Of course, no such conspiracy existed. True, Heine's fundamental criticism of contemporary society, expressed as it was in a captivating, racy, and novel style, made him the model for the new generation of writers. The other leading figure was Ludwig Börne who, curiously enough, was not included in the ban, perhaps because his polemic was mainly political, without the religious and sexual overtones that were considered especially objectionable. Then as now, censors seem to think of morality mainly in terms of sexual morality.

There has been some dispute on the practical effectiveness of a draconic edict which would ban not only existing works but future ones as well. Suffice it to say, Heine continued to write and Campe continued to publish his works. "Ich bin nicht dazu geeignet, ein Kerkermeister der Gedanken zu sein" ("I am not suited to act as a jailer of ideas," 5:258), he had said in *Romantische Schule*. The specter of censorship never ceased to loom large in his consciousness, causing him to complain bitterly that it interfered with the pursuit of his innermost calling as well as of his livelihood—which was precisely what was intended: it also challenged him to respond—as he always did in the face of adversity—with choice flashes of wit. Still, for the time being he accommodated himself to the circumstances by writing on seemingly innocuous topics (for instance, "Elementargeister,") and by turning to fiction.

Narrative Fiction

One of the more harmless projects was the novella *Florentinische Nächte* [Florentine Nights], an amalgam of short tales with which the narrator Maximilian attempts to distract and amuse his friend Maria, who is dying of consumption. This blend of love and death also permeates the stories themselves, in which the narrator tells of falling in love with a marble statue, a gothic portrait, and finally, in the most fantastic episode of all, with a strange young woman whom he first observed performing a Bacchanalian dance on the streets of London (4:149). He makes love to her after he encounters her again in a Paris salon, as wife of a French nobleman. It is then he also learns the macabre story of her background. Her pregnant mother, maltreated by her husband, the count, had fallen into a coma and, presumed dead, was buried in great splendor. Grave robbers find her in labor and, having reburied the mother who is now irrevocably dead, leave with the baby girl whom they nickname "Totenkind" ("child of death").

The ailing Maria evidently needs strong medicine to keep her interest alive! Another starkly memorable episode describes a concert by Paganini. Here Heine transposes the reportedly satanic power of Paganini's violin into language—a feat which brings to mind similar passages in Thomas Mann's *Death in Venice* or *Doctor Faustus*. The parallel may not be altogether coincidental. What seems to emerge as a dominant theme in the bizarre episodes of *Florentinische Nächte*—as it does in Mann—is the dark, demonic side of art, the melding of beauty and horror, in short, the Dionysian aspect of aesthetic experience. In contrast to the Apollonian serenity and contained formality associated with Goethe's classical concept, this was a revelation which earned Heine the reputation of having introduced the Dionysian theme into German literature.[1]

For a touch of realism and comic relief the novella includes some of Heine's unflattering observations on the English, as encountered en route or remembered from his visit. On their speech: "They stuff a dozen monosyllables into their mouths, chew them up, squash them and spit them out again, and they call that talking . . ." (4:142). With regard to their culinary preferences—which he considers to be telling indicators of personality and character: "These roasts of beef and mutton are the only good things they have. Heaven preserve all good Christians from their sauces, which consist of one third flour and two thirds butter, or, should variety be desired, of one third butter and two thirds flour. Heaven preserve us also from their naive vegetables, which they boil in water and bring to the table just as God created them" (4:143).

Among the unfinished manuscripts which Heine had brought to Paris was the opening chapter of *Der Rabbi von Bacharach* [The Rabbi of Bacharach]. He had written it following his sojourn in Berlin, where his association with the Jewish reform group had awakened his interest in his own roots. What he had in mind was a historical novel about the Jews, in the manner of Walter Scott: *Ein mittelalterliches Sittenbild,* a medieval portrayal of customs and mores, he called it later. Set in the fifteenth century, in the Rhenish town of Bacharach, it indeed begins like a period piece, with the description of a celebration of Passover. The Seder is conducted by Rabbi Abraham, a cultured Jew recently returned from studies in Spain. Almost at once, the religious idyll is invaded by horror as the rabbi, already somewhat puzzled by the presence of two strangers, notices a child's corpse under the table: the strangers had smuggled it in to accuse the Jews of ritual murder and to instigate a pogrom. The rabbi and his wife, "the beautiful Sara," manage to escape, and after a romantic, moonlit journey up the Rhine, they take refuge in the Frankfurt ghetto. Beautiful and poignant, the episode is seriously flawed by Heine's failure to justify the apparent irresponsibility with which the rabbi deserts his congregation while seeking his and his wife's safety. But in spite of this weakness, the piece starkly conveys the vulnerability of the small Jewish community amid hostile surroundings. (It is worth remembering that Heine's later decision to continue the story and publish it, albeit still a fragment, was brought about by reports of a similar incident in contemporary Damascus, where Jews were persecuted in the wake of allegations of ritual murder.)

The Frankfurt ghetto affords relative security. With the change of scene, the tone and mode abruptly shifts from the moving romance of

Jewish martyrdom to a good-natured, robust satire on life in the ghetto. These passages, probably written after a fifteen-year interval, underscore the absurdity of ghetto isolation and the barrier of fear. They poke fun at the religious ritual and whimsically sketch the foibles and eccentricities of individual figures. Throughout, one can practically smell and taste the aroma of Jewish holiday fare.

This lure of Jewish cooking—Heine elsewhere calls it *Kuhreigen der Juden,* likening it to the powerful tune with which Alpine shepherds call their herd—forms the link with the even more farcical last chapter. Here a new arrival to the ghetto is introduced, the urbane, flamboyant Don Isaak, just returned from Spain. With irony and unmistakable self-parody, Heine presents the glib talking, flirtatious knight, a sophisticated renegade from Judaism who is enticed back to the ghetto by the memory of carp in raisin sauce and mutton with garlic.

The serious concern beneath the farce is with the nature of the bond which keeps modern Judaism alive. Heine considers the cultural pull to be much stronger than theological doctrine.

The *Rabbi* was the first of Heine's narrative projects to be undertaken and the last to be published (*Salon,* volume 4). A previous attempt at writing narrative fiction had appeared in *Salon,* volume 1 (1834), which puts its origin in the vicinity of the great historical essays—a vicinity which, it turns out, is reflected in its central theme. The title—*Aus den Memoiren des Herrn von Schnabelewopski* [From the Memoirs of Sir Schnabelewopski]—and the opening sentence give a hint of the parodistic intent of what in effect is an experiment with the picaresque format: "My father's name was Schnabelewops, my mother's name was Schnabelewopska and I, legitimate son of both of them, was born at Schnabelewops in Poland on April 1, 1795" (4:53). In due course, the hero—whose voice throughout is often not distinguishable from that of the author—sets out to see the world, with a first stopover in Hamburg. This is the occasion for one of Heine's most rollicking satires on the Hamburg scene, especially on the Jewish Philistine merchants. From there the hero proceeds to Amsterdam and Leiden. He takes up residence in a house formerly inhabited by the Dutch realist painter Jan Steen whose joyous, earthy vitality epitomizes the most positive aspect of sensualism: "No nightingale ever has sung as cheerfully and jubilantly as Jan Steen has painted. Nobody has understood as profoundly as he that there ought to be eternal carnival [*Kirmes*] on this earth; he understood that our life is only a colorful kiss of God, and he knew that the Holy Ghost reveals itself most gloriously in light and laughter" (4:93).

This exuberant affirmation of life which radiates from Steen's paintings, not to be confused with the mindless self-indulgent materialism that had been the butt of the Hamburg lampoon, sharply contrasts with the repressive asceticism that dominates the life of the home's occupants. The landlord, a maker of hernia trusses, is a fanatical Anabaptist whose sole pleasure and sexual outlet is provided through his dreams, when he keeps company with the beautiful ladies of the Bible. As he reports his nightly fantasies to his spouse over breakfast, she is consumed with jealousy. Why can he not stick to the virgin Mary, or old Martha, or even Magdalena who, after all, reformed in the end? But to hobnob with that Madame Judith, or the wayward Queen of Sheba! When "Mynheer" divulges that the beautiful Esther had called on him to assist her with her toilet (to dress or undress?—"bei ihrer Toilette behilflich sein" admits both options) "to win over King Ahasverus for the good cause," the wife is beside herself with jealous fury and lashes him with his trusses (4:96) The ensuing reflection on dreams is as intriguing as it is perceptive. In defining their function psychologically, as an outlet for repressed emotions, Heine seems to anticipate Freud and Jung.

The landlady's frustration in turn has unfortunate consequences. "Had she been Italian, she might have poisoned my food. Being Dutch, she sent me up a very bad meal" (4:100). His fellow sufferers are three other boarders whose discussions on theological-philosophical subjects our hero has been following. The trio consists of a Jewish theist named Simson, a robust Friesian freethinker, and a disciple of Fichte. As the quality of the meals deteriorates, their argument about the existence of God becomes more heated, finally leading to a duel between the theist and the freethinker in which the theist succumbs. Mindful of the feat of his biblical namesake whose strength of belief shook the pillars of the temple, pathetic little Simson shakes the bedposts—but to no avail. As blood gushes from his heart, he realizes that his God has lost his power.

The mood has drastically changed from the buffoonery with which the piece began. Here as elsewhere when he notes that Jehovah is dead, Heine registers nostalgic regret—although his reason and sense of justice bid him welcome advancing secularization and humanist orientation. Buried under the burlesque surface of this seemingly casual romp is the persistent concern with liberation from ascetic repression, in this instance with emphasis on personal and psychological rather than political implications. While the actual plot—if one exists at all—simply consists in the narrative persona's experiences and observations, the thematic network is intricate and complicated. The attempt to uncover how each episode relates to the central theme poses an interesting challenge to the reader.

The above reference to Esther's attempt to "win King Ahasverus for the good cause" alludes to an episode in *Schnabelewopski* which constitutes the best-known part of the fragment. During his stay in Amsterdam, the narrator claims to have attended a performance of *Der fliegende Holländer* [The Flying Dutchman]. Heine previously mentioned this tale in *Nordsee* (3:100). Now he elaborates, giving his personal version, complete with a characteristically ironic twist at the end. The Flying Dutchman (alias King Ahasverus, the wandering Jew) can only find release from his eternal wanderings through the loyalty of a loving woman. Women in love are not difficult to come by—but eternal loyalty? Heine at last has the grisly old man of the sea saved through the love of the devoted Katharina. However, as the only certain way of ensuring her own faithfulness, she commits suicide. Richard Wagner's opera is based on Heine's tale. Although the anti-Semitic Wagner was reluctant to acknowledge his debt to the Jew Heine for themes from Germany mythology,[2] there can be little doubt that in several instances, in addition to those already mentioned, he found the source of his inspiration in Heine's work. The opera *Götterdämmerung* [Twilight of the Gods] owes its title to Heine's poem of the same name (1:148). And it is probably no coincidence that Wagner's choice of medieval themes fell on the ones which had been singled out for special praise and attention in *Romantische Schule* (Die Nibelungen, Parcifal, Tristan) and in "Elementargeister" (Lohengrin as well as Tannhäuser).

Dramatic Attempts

Evidence of Heine's creative imagination may be found on just about every page of his essayistic and journalistic oeuvre, not to mention his poetry. Yet, strangely enough, his efforts to sustain the fictional mode do not appear to have been successful. This applies to his youthful dramatic attempts as much as to his narrative fiction. At the time when he was composing some of the poetry which was destined to establish his international reputation as a leading German lyricist, his hopes actually centered on two tragedies. *Almansor,* on which he labored while he was a student at Bonn and Göttingen, and *William Ratcliff,* quickly created while he was studying in Berlin, were published in 1823, together with "Lyrisches Intermezzo."

Both dramas have unhappy love for their major theme. *Almansor* which echoes motifs from both *Romeo and Juliet* and Lessing's *Nathan der Weise,* is set in Granada, Spain. The star-crossed lovers, Almansor and Zuleima, are kept apart not by their feuding families but by religion. The (noble) Moor Almansor resists conversion to the Christian faith of his beloved Zuleima. That they had been switched as babies and consequently were not brought up in the religion of their natural parents, underlines still further the absurdity and arbitrariness of religious divison and strife. It goes without saying that the problems arising from the gulf between Christianity and Islam provide a but thinly disguised metaphor for the situation close to the poet's heart and his very personal grievance; his sympathetic appreciation of Moorish attitudes, under pressure from Christian self-righteous intransigence, must have been provocatively transparent to his contemporaries.

If the tone of *Almansor* is lyrical-elegiac, *William Ratcliff* is a tight, blood-and-thunder melodrama, patterned on the romantic *Schicksalstragödie* ("fate tragedy") where the life of the protagonists inexorably follows a preordained path till all the participants have met violent deaths. Heine's drama is set in a gloomy Scottish castle, the action is fast-paced and stark, the atmosphere foggy and ominous, and the final pileup of corpses impressive. William Ratcliff, turned down by the beautiful Maria McGregor, vows to kill her successful suitors. He has already disposed of two bridegrooms (who seem to turn up at two-year intervals). After each murder he has returned the bloodied ring to the betrothed. But the third suitor frustrates his intent by actually saving his, William Ratcliff's, life. Since gratitude prevents him from killing his rival, there is no other way out but to kill himself, along with Maria and her father—all of which was predestined to happen and was in fact manipulated by the ghosts of Maria's mother and William's father, who make repeated appearances throughout the bloody proceedings, having been, as it turns out, illicit lovers in their

time. *Almansor* and *William Ratcliff* are both written in the classical
pentameter. *Almansor* was produced once in Heine's time (predictably,
without much success) but the author was unable to persuade
anyone—including his friend Laube when he became director of the
Burgtheater in Vienna—to undertake a production of *William Ratcliff.*
However, it subsequently provided libretti for operas by César Cui
(1869) and Pietro Mascagni (1895).

Ballet Scenarios

From the beginning of his career, Heine was interested in the dance
as a primal expression of human emotions; and the theme of dance not
only pervades his poetry[3] but crops up again and again in his prose as
well, from *Reisebilder* to *Florentinische Nächte* and *Elementargeister,* not to
forget that the hero of *Atta Troll* is a dancing bear. His tale of the
dancing *Willis* (brides who died before their wedding and who return to
dance their lovers to death), contained in *Elementargeister,* was to form
the basis of Adolphe Adam's ballet *Gisèlle* which had its Paris première
in 1841 and has remained one of the most popular numbers in the
international ballet repertory ever since. Thus, when Benjamin Lumley, director of Her Majesty's Ballet in London, invited Heine to submit
some ballet scenarios, he was happy to oblige with *Die Göttin Diana*
[The Goddess Diana, 1846] and *Der Doktor Faust* (1847).

Heine's Diana bears little resemblance to Apollo's cool sister, the
classical guardian of chastity. On the contrary, in his treatment she has
turned into a wanton seductress, eager to make up for the pleasures she
has missed during her existence in antiquity.[4] In the ballet sketch, her
encounter with an idealistic German knight serves to convey the
polarity of spiritualism and sensualism which never ceased to interest
Heine.

The same basic conflict forms the theme of *Der Doktor Faust,* as the
author explains at length in the introductory "letter," or essay, on the
significance of the Faust theme. It contains, not surprisingly, one
further, final, response to Goethe. In Heine's view, the Faust legend
constitutes the supreme expression of the spiritual-sensual dichotomy,
but he claims that the traditional version of the medieval chapbook
comes more profoundly to grips with the theme than Goethe's treatment. His own provocative innovation—consistent with his view of

womanhood as well as with his sense of irony, perhaps also with the wish to play one last trick on Goethe—is the introduction of Mephistophela, the female Satan. Instead of the "eternal feminine" which, in Goethe's masterpiece, intervenes to save Faust from damnation, Heine's Mephistophela ultimately defeats him.

Some scholars look on Heine's *Der Doktor Faust* as an important, original contribution to the Faust literature.[5] Neither ballet was successfully performed, at least not until the German composer Werner Egk set Heine's Faust scenario to music in his ballet *Abraxas*.[6] Egk's ballet was first performed in Munich in 1948—one hundred years after the publication of Heine's work—but after one performance it was banned by the Bavarian government because of its frank treatment of sex. Nevertheless in the following season, fifty performances were given in Berlin with great success.

Chapter Six
The Mock Epics

Atta Troll. A Midsummer Night's Dream

These first lines of the third canto announce the poet's intention regarding *Atta Troll. Ein Sommernachtstraum* [Atta Troll: A Midsummer Night's Dream]:

> Traum der Sommernacht! Phantastisch
> Zwecklos ist mein Lied. Ja, zwecklos
> Wie die Liebe, wie das Leben,
> Wie der Schöpfer samt der Schöpfung!

> Dream of a summer night! Fantastic,
> Without purpose is my song. Yes, without purpose,
> Like love, like life
> Like the creator and his creation. (1:354)

His beloved Pegasus is to be allowed free reign. It is to be the swan song of a declining age, "das letzte freie Waldlied der Romantik" ("the last free woodland song of Romanticism"). Begun in 1841, this first major project since the Börne book in a sense follows from it logically. There, Heine made the case for the independent, "autonomous" artist—albeit one with a feel for the pulse of the time—in contrast to the political publicist and activist. He now demonstrates his independence by an excursion into the land of pure fantasy and provocatively places his whimsy in the broadest possible context: "zwecklos ist mein Lied, wie das Leben, wie . . . (die) Schöpfung." Compressed into this sweeping remark, his existentialist declaration, running counter to religious beliefs and idealist optimism, must have seemed shocking to some. Yet Heine probably merely wished to distance himself from his literary colleagues whom he accused of placing their muse at the service of partisan causes. But even while defending his right to create "useless" poetry that follows its own internal law, he raised this independence to a cause. The mock epic *Atta Troll,* studded with barbs against *Tendenzdichter,* activist writers who advocated worthy causes with second-rate poetry, is itself brimming with topical and political cross-references.

The poet's fortunes were at a low ebb at the time. Assailed and berated on all sides in the wake of the Börne book uproar, he also began to have serious problems with his health. The headaches returned, he experienced eye troubles, and he had the first attacks of the paralysis which was to cripple him later. Yet *Atta Troll* is one of the most charming and seemingly lighthearted works. Begun while he was recuperating in Cauterets, a spa in the Pyrenées, the epic was first published as a fragment in 1843 and appeared in its final version as a book in 1847, although even then the author felt that it was unfinished: "Like all great German works" he quipped in the introduction, "like the Cathedral of Cologne, Schelling's God, the Prussian constitution[1]—it has not been completed" (1:343).

Atta Troll consists of twenty-seven cantos made up of four-line stanzas. But the reader is likely to be well into the poem before noting that these trochaic tetrameters, with their peculiarly compelling cadences, do not rhyme. The plot is simple. It is the story of the dancing bear who escapes his keeper and returns to the wild. His escape and the ensuing attempts at hunting him down form the framework for a loosely linked chain of episodes. At first we follow the bear to his cave and observe him as he pontificates to his young about the state of the world, and then we accompany the hunter, together with the mysterious mute Laskaro, on his varied adventures, over hills and dales, through villages and caves of the Pyrenées. The scenic background of this fantastic journey seems palpably real, beginning with the spectacular mountain scene with which it opens:

> Rings umragt von dunklen Bergen
> Die sich trotzig übergipfeln,
> Und von wilden Wasserstürzen
> Eingelullet, wie ein Traumbild,
>
> Liegt im Tal das elegante
> Cauterets. Die weissen Häuschen
> Mit Balkonen; schöne Damen
> Stehn darauf und lachen herzlich. (canto 1; 1:349)

(Surrounded by dark mountains
Defiantly towering over one another
And by wild waterfalls,
Lulled asleep, like a dream image,

The elegant Cauterets lies in the
Valley. White little houses,
With balconies; beautiful ladies
Standing there, laughing heartily.)

This is the frame, almost literally the viewing post, from which at the outset the action is being observed: the pretty ladies, amused by the antics of the bears below, also represent the society which Atta Troll mocks. Other starkly realistic settings form the frames to canto: 13–15, in each case preparing the reader for the adventure of the particular day—or, as in this instance, the night:

In dem schwarzen Felsenkessel
Ruht der See, das tiefe Wasser.
Melancholisch bleiche Sterne
Schaun vom Himmel. Nacht und Stille.

Nacht und Stille. Ruderschläge.
Wie ein plätscherndes Geheimnis
Schwimmt der Kahn. Des Fährmanns Rolle
Übernahmen seine Nichten. (1:380)

(In the black rock canyon
Rests the lake, the deep water.
Melancholy, pale stars
Look down from the sky. Night and stillness.

Night and stillness. The beat of oars.
Like a splashing secret
The boat glides. The ferryman's role
Was taken over by his nieces.)

The nieces now claim the persona's attention. Are they real, or water sprites, figments of his imagination? After the appropriate test, he comes to the rational conclusion (*Vernunftschluss*): "Ja, ich küsse, also leb' ich!" ("Yes, I am kissing, therefore I am alive")—a clever paraphrase of the Cartesian dictum. Sun-lit scenes materialize equally convincingly. What visitor to the mountains does not recognize the following view:

> Aus dem sonn 'gen Goldgrund lachen
> Violette Bergeshöhen,
> Und am Abhang klebt ein Dörfchen
> Wie ein keckes Vogelnest. (canto 14; 1:381–82)

> (Out of the sunny gold-ground smile
> Violet hills,
> And stuck onto the hillside is a little village,
> Like a cheeky bird's nest.)

The high-spirited, happy mood exuding from this quatrain, conveyed by its sound and rhythm as much as by the meaning of its words, is matched by the experience which follows: the two men find themselves greeted by a group of playing, dancing children. "Girofflino, Girofflette" sounds the endearing refrain of their round, and:

> Während ich ins Tal hinabstieg,
> Scholl mir nach, verhallend lieblich,
> Immerfort, wie Vogelzwitschern:
> "Girofflino, Girofflette!" (canto 14, 1:384)

> (As I descended into the valley
> The sounds followed me, sweetly lingering
> Like the twitter of birds:
> Girofflino, Girofflette!)

This refrain, it is said, may still be heard in one of the Pyrenées valleys (Giroflé is the name of a flower).

Also likely to remain in the reader's mind is the poet's capricious dialogue, with the snow, high up on the mountain, followed by an intense scene which silhouettes the sinister figure of Laskaro against the snowy waste, the tall feather from the bird he had just shot slowly moving back and forth on the hunter's hat (canto 16; 1:386f.).

Heine's contemporaries must have chuckled over the many witty connections with events and figures of the day. Some of them are dated while the effect of others has not paled. The reference to one ever-present personage—or rather, to the bear's notion of him—has not lost its effectiveness. This is how Atta Troll describes his deity in one telling, impressive stanza:

> Droben in dem Sternenzelte,
> Auf dem goldnen Herrscherstuhle,
> Weltregierend, majestätisch,
> Sitzt ein kolossaler Eisbär. (canto 8; 1:368)

> (High up in the celestial vault,
> On the golden throne,
> With majesty reigning over the universe,
> There sits a colossal polar bear.)

Has Ludwig Feuerbach's thesis that man creates gods in his image ever been stated more concisely? Or our conventional theology been more disarmingly lampooned?

Critics have occasionally wondered who is actually meant by the bear Atta Troll. Is it Ludwig Börne? Indeed, Atta Troll often sounds like a radical republican of Börne's persuasion, and while his epitaph, with its reference to the polarity of talent and character, pokes fun at Börne, his is by no means a single voice or uniform perspective. Rather, he seems to serve as a mouthpiece for the author's satiric barbs in whatever direction they may be aimed. Some of Heine's best ironic effects are achieved by imitating the voice of his victims. In the following excerpt, Atta Troll speaks in the manner of the self-righteous citizen, his ever-lurking anti-Semitism only superficially covered by his lofty ideals, his self-interest fully intact and coated in pompous rationalization. Atta Troll has just postulated that in his ideal state there would be complete equality between all creatures, with inalienable rights guaranteed to all, when he attaches one proviso:

> Ja, sogar die Juden sollen
> Volles Bürgerrecht geniessen
> Und gesetzlich gleichgestellt sein
> Allen andern Säugetieren.

> Nur das Tanzen auf den Märkten
> Sei den Juden nicht gestattet;
> Dies Amendement, ich mach es
> Im Intresse meiner Kunst. (canto 6; 1:364)

(Yes, even the Jews are
To enjoy full rights of citizenship
And equality before the law
With all other mammals.

Only the dancing on the market.
Must not be permitted to Jews.
I am making this amendment
In the interest of my art.)

Midsummer night's dream culminates in midsummer night's madness in the spook of the *Wilde Jagd* ("wild hunt" or "ghostly chase") at midnight of St. John's day. In Heine's version of *Walpurgisnacht*,[2] illustrious specters from the past charge by in a phantasmagoric chase. Outstanding amid the assorted celebrities (which include Shakespeare and Goethe, both pursued by their respective commentators, who are mounted on asses to which they frantically cling) are three beautiful female apparitions: the sensual Diana, the laughing Abunde, and the darkly beckoning Herodias. This lovely trio embodies three kinds of feminine lure but also, and more importantly, it symbolizes the three strands of tradition prevailing in the author's cultural heritage: the Hellenic, the Teutonic-Celtic, and the Judaic. Significantly, he endows Herodias—seen playing ball with the severed head of St. John—with the most powerful mystique. The theme of the blood-thirsty eroticism of Herodias-Salome, as introduced here by Heine, has been taken up repeatedly by the French symbolists[3] and still lives on as immortalized by Oscar Wilde and Richard Strauss in *Salome*.

Germany. A Winter's Tale

In October, 1843, and again the following July, Heine dared to return to Germany for several weeks. The journey was not without risks. While he had come to Paris on his own initiative, his exile by now was no longer voluntary. The Prussian authorities had issued a warrant for his arrest, and Prussian territory at that time began at the banks of the Rhine. Several reasons impelled him to undertake the trip nevertheless. Foremost in his mind was his concern for his seventy-two-year-old mother, who was in failing health and whose home had been destroyed in Hamburg's great fire of 1842. There were financial matters to be discussed with Uncle Salomon. He expected to be remembered in the millionaire banker's will and was anxious to ensure continued support for his wife Mathilde after his own death. No less important seemed a face-to-face meeting with Julius Campe, with whom Heine had long since planned to bring out a collected edition of his works. This project, unfortunately, did not materialize in his lifetime. But for once he was able to supervise the production of one of his works, namely, a new volume of poems. Having planned *Neue Gedichte* during his first sojourn, he was able to see it through the press during his second visit. Last but not least, he simply needed to renew contact with Germany, to hear the German language and breathe German air, and even to savor, as he put it, German *Dummheiten* ("follies").

Just how stimulating the contact turned out to be is manifest in the mock-epic *Deutschland. Ein Wintermärchen* [Germany: A Winter's Tale]. As Heine said himself, alluding to the myth of Antaeus whose strength was restored whenever he touched (his mother) earth:

> Seit ich auf deutsche Erde trat,
> Durchströmen mich Zaubersäfte—
> Der Riese hat wieder die Mutter berührt,
> Und es wuchsen ihm neu die Kräfte. (1:437)

> (As soon as I stepped on German soil,
> Magic juices flooded through me—
> The giant once again touched his mother,
> And his strength grew anew.)

The poem was completed within six weeks after his return, and ready to be included in *Neue Gedichte*. Within the same year it appeared in two more editions. The Paris *Vorwärts!* [Advance!] a short-lived radical journal which Marx had taken over, published the poem in installments, and Campe also produced it as a separate publication, preceded by a preface which contains—as so many of Heine's introductions do—an eloquent defense of his lone, embattled position. Here he fends off the charge that he lacks patriotism. As is his wont, he counters by turning the accusation around, claiming for himself a broader and truer vision than his nationalist detractors are capable of:

I can already hear their beery voices: "You even blaspheme our colors, you defamer of the fatherland and friend of the French, to whom you would yield our free Rhine!" Calm yourselves. I will regard and respect your colors when they deserve it, when they are no longer merely an idle or servile plaything. Hoist the black, red, and gold banner on the heights of German thought. Make it the emblem of free humanity and I will give my best heart's blood for it. . . . The people of Alsace Lorraine will once more join Germany if we complete what the French have begun . . . if we destroy servitude everywhere, even in its last place of refuge, in heaven, if we redeem the God who dwells on earth within man, if we become God's redeemers, if we restore to dignity the poor people that have been deprived of their heritage of happiness. . . . Yes, then not merely Alsace and Lorraine, but the whole of Germany will become ours, the whole of Europe, the whole world—the whole world will become German. Of this mission and universal sovereignty of Germany I often dream when walking under oak trees. That is *my* patriotism. (1:432–33)

In East Germany, *Deutschland. Ein Wintermärchen* is prized not only as Heine's most important work but as one of the supreme achievements in German literature, outranked only by Goethe's *Faust*. Elsewhere, it is regarded as Germany's chief political poem—not that there is much competition—and certainly the funniest.

It is a versified travelogue. The seemingly endless column of quatrains, in the familiar folksong format with rhymed second and fourth lines, is divided into twenty-seven segments—as in Atta Troll, Heine uses the designation *caput* ("canto"). The fictitious journey (reversing the route which Heine had actually taken) provides the framework for a plethora of scenes: satirical or simply amusing, beautiful or touching, tender or coarse, profound or trivial. Enveloping them all is the mood of sparkling good humor. Heine's presence as the narrator is dominant, the tone direct and colloquial, aimed at a broad audience. There is nothing impenetrable or obscure about this poem—which is not to say that it does not have some subtly ambivalent moments (e.g., the scene in Cologne, cantos 6–7). The rhymes include some outrageously comical concoctions. With the illuminating flash of wit, Heine throws into relief the absurdity of many situations and phenomena.

The main target is not so much Germany as a whole but Prussia: Prussian militarism, the attempts at reviving obsolete medieval institutions, romantic obscurantism, economic backwardness, political apathy and servility, as well as assorted literary quarry. However, it is important to keep in mind what *Deutschland* does not contain: although it represents the sort of attitude which later in the century has spawned political and social programs of reform, it does not propose such a program.[4] As always, Heine is very clear about the targets of his criticism but less articulate—or specific—about the positive goals to be achieved. Invariably the revolutionary ideal as projected by him is imbued with a mythological aura.[5]

> Im traurigen Monat November war's,
> Die Tage wurden trüber,
> Der Wind riss von den Bäumen das Laub,
> Da reist ich nach Deutschland hinüber. (1:435)

> (In the dreary month of November it was
> The days were getting duller,
> The wind tore the leaves off the trees,
> Then I traveled across to Germany.)

Thus Heine introduces his journey, setting the scene and creating a mood with four terse statements. Presently the traveler hears a young harpist sing, the first sounds in his mother tongue since crossing the border: "Sie sang mit wahrem Gefühle und falscher Stimme" ("she sang with true feeling and in an off-key voice"). It is a brilliant opening! The traveler notes her sentimental lament, her message of renunciation and sacrifice, coupled with the expectation of paradisiacal solace and bliss in the hereafter, and he counters with the promise of a "new and better song":

> Sie sang das alte Entsagungslied,
> Das Eiapopeia vom Himmel,
> Womit man einlullt, wenn es greint,
> Das Volk, den grossen Lümmel. (1:436)

> (She sang the old song of renunciation,
> The Eiapopeia about heaven,
> With which they lull the people to sleep
> When it cries, that big slouch.)

> Ein neues Lied, ein besseres Lied,
> O Freunde, will ich euch dichten!
> Wir wollen hier auf Erden schon
> Das Himmelreich errichten.

. . . .

Es wächst hienieden Brot genug
Für alle Menschenkinder,
Auch Rosen und Myrten, Schönheit und Lust,
Und Zuckererbsen nicht minder.

Ja, Zuckererbsen für jedermann,
Sobald die Schoten platzen!
Den Himmel überlassen wir
Den Engeln und den Spatzen. (canto 1; 1:436)

(A new song, a better song,
My friends, I shall compose for you!
Here on this earth let us
Found the heavenly realm.

. . . .

There grows enough bread down here
For all mankind
As well as roses and myrtle, beauty and joy
And even sugar-peas.

Yes, sugar-peas for everyone,
As soon as the pods are bursting!
The heaven [or skies—"Himmel" means both] we gladly leave
For the angels and the sparrows.)

These famous lines hardly require any comment—except perhaps to point out once more the author's consummate skill in condensing thought into graphic and radiant images. Who but Heine could be so concrete in his specifications of the ingredients of all-inclusive pleasure! Modern readers in the Western world will smile to see *Zuckererbsen* ("peas") singled out as the gourmand's ultimate delight: it is one prophecy where even Heine, with his penchant for hyperbole and utopic goals, did not, as it turned out, promise too much. Frozen peas are a standby in North American kitchens.

Toward the end of the poem, the author returns to the confident optimism about a better life, based on the emergence of a new kind of man who is emancipated from the burden of guilt and neurotic repression. It is a statement which anticipates Nietzsche's notion of superman and the call for renewal as enunciated by the expressionists:

Das alte Geschlecht der Heuchelei
Verschwindet, Gott sei Dank, heut,
es sinkt allmählich ins Grab, es stirbt
an seiner Lügenkrankheit.

Es wächst heran ein neues Geschlecht,
Ganz ohne Schminke und Sünden,
Mit freien Gedanken, mit freier Lust—
Dem werde ich alles verkünden. (canto 27; 1:504)

(The old dissembling generation
Is now, thank God, disappearing,
Gradually sinking into the grave, dying
Of its sickness of hypocrisy.

A new generation is growing up,
Quite without pretense (makeup) and sin,
With free thought, with free joy—
To it I shall reveal it all.)

This lofty promise will be preceded by a revelation of a different kind. Hammonia had just given the traveler a preview of Germany's future by letting him see—and smell—the contents of her apocalyptic chamber pot. Even devoted fans of *Deutschland. Ein Wintermärchen* must find these passages crude and tasteless. In the past, this section tended to be relegated to the commentary by protective editors—unless the censor had already taken care of them altogether.

These prophecies—at the outset and end of the trip—form a frame; and by implication also a frame of reference. Apart from it, the thread of coherence is supplied by the critique contained in the ironic and satiric mode.

Customs inspection offers an opportunity for a quick shift after the earnest mood of canto 1. The Prussian customs officers who are rummaging through the traveler's trunk in search of subversive material inspire these thoughts:

Ihr Toren, die ihr im Koffer sucht!
Hier werdet ihr nichts entdecken!
Die Konterbande, die mit mir reist,
Die hab ich im Kopfe stecken. (1:438)

(You fools who are searching my suitcase!
Here you will find nothing!
The forbidden goods that travel with me
Are hidden inside my head.)

On the subject of customs, a fellow passenger is credited with this
observation:

"Der Zollverein"—bemerkte er—
"Wird unser Volkstum begründen,
Er wird das zersplitterte Vaterland
Zu einem Ganzen verbinden.

Er gibt die äussere Einheit uns,
Die sogenannt materielle;
Die geistige Einheit gibt uns die Zensur,
Die wahrhaft ideelle—

Sie gibt die innere Einheit uns,
Die Einheit im Denken und Sinnen;
Ein einiges Deutschland tut uns not,
Einig nach aussen und innen." (1:439)

("Customs union"—he remarked—
"Will found our nationhood,
And will unite our splintered fatherland
Into a whole.

It gives us an external unity,
The so-called material one;
Censorship gives us the intellectual unity,
The truly spiritual one—

It gives us the internal unity,
Unity of thought and mind;
We do need a united Germany,
United externally and internally.")

The didactic tone of the solid, earnest patriot and the seemingly
compelling logic with which he links customs union and censorship as a
sure way to national unity add up to a supreme piece of irony. Heine's

joke has not lost its import for our times when solemn censors still occasionally try to promote the kind of "internal, spiritual unity" which he lampooned.

Strolling through Aachen where Charlemagne—epitome of greatness and style—lies buried, Heine observes the Prussian military, takes note of their changed uniforms, and muses about their unchanged rigidity of posture:

Sie stelzen noch immer so steif herum,
So kerzengrade geschniegelt,
Als hätten sie verschluckt den Stock,
Womit man sie einst geprügelt. (canto 3; 1:440)

(They are still strutting so stiffly,
So ramrod straight and polished,
As if they had swallowed the stick
With which they used to be beaten.)

What modern psychologists term the process of internalization seems here captured and diagnosed with graphic accuracy! Contemporaries, knowing that the *Zopf* ("pigtail") had recently been abandoned as part of the Prussian military costume, and familiar with the pejorative connotation of the word in connection with outmoded convention and narrow-minded rigidity, must have been delighted with these lines:

Der lange Schnurrbart ist eigentlich nur
Des Zopftums neuere Phase:
Der Zopf, der eh'mals hinten hing,
Der hängt jetzt unter der Nase. (canto 3; 1:440)

(The long moustache is actually only
The new phase of "Zopf" mentality;
The Zopf which used to hang behind,
Now hangs underneath the nose.)

In Cologne, Heine has a charming conversation with his beloved Father Rhine who tells him that he, too, has missed him these last twelve years, and catches him up on some of his more recent complaints; the song by Nikolaus Becker[6] he finds especially difficult to swallow, more difficult even than the stones at Biberach. This is a reminder of the 1841 feud between Nassau and Rheinhessen, in the course of which several ship loads of stone were dumped into the Rhine to eliminate the competition of Mainz as a harbor.

Thus Heine incessantly finds connections between seemingly unrelated phenomena, establishes parallels, relationships, allusions, and links where most people would not expect them, and the reader is challenged and delighted to follow him on the intellectual journey.

The sojourn in Cologne yields another encounter. Wandering through the deserted, moon-lit streets, the poet finds himself followed by a mysterious figure. The scene calls to mind a similar experience ("Heimkehr", 20; 1:115) when he was haunted by the specter of his past. But this is a shadowy companion of another kind. "Ich bin kein Gespenst der Vergangenheit" ("I am no specter of the past"), he introduces himself, "Ich bin von praktischer Natur, und immer schweigsam und ruhig. Doch wisse: was du ersonnen im Geist, das führ ich aus, das tu ich" ("I am of a practical nature, and always silent and quiet. Yet know: what you have thought up with your mind, I carry it out, I do it"). That very night, the poet dreams that he is visiting the three Magi in the cathedral—the Holy Kings had been mentioned in the preceding canto as symbols of absolute power and romantic glory—and he finds that the skeletons are preparing to reenter the world of the living. They demand respect due to kings, the saints, and the dead. Cheerfully asserting the claims of life and dominance of the present over the obsolete past, the poet remonstrates, when all of a sudden his *lictor,* the ghostly hatchet man, appears at his side:

> Er nahte sich, und mit dem Beil
> Zerschmetterte er die armen
> Skelette des Aberglaubens, er schlug
> Sie nieder ohn' Erbarmen.

> Es dröhnte der Hiebe Widerhall
> Aus allen Gewölben, entsetzlich!—
> Blutströme schossen aus meiner Brust,
> Und ich erwachte plötzlich. (1:455)

> (He approached, and with his sword
> He shattered the poor
> Skeletons of superstition, he cut
> Them down without pity.

> The echo of his blows
> Horribly resounded from all the vaults!—
> Blood flowed from my chest,
> And suddenly I awoke.)

The meaning is unmistakable in its manifold aspects: the belief in the practical consequences of ideas and in the poet's commitment to serve the interests of the present, coupled with the dilemma of one who resents the obscurantist revival of relics yet whose own tap roots are deeply embedded in romantic tradition.

Passing through the Teutoburger Wald (Teutoburg Forest) the traveler reflects what the consequences might have been if the Romans rather than Hermann (Arminius) had been victorious in the great battle of 9 A.D. This very amusing canto (11) did not make many friends among German patriots.

We actually get very few realistic glimpses of German landscape and people, aside from the periodic reports on the weather, the comfort or discomfort of travel (mostly the latter), and the rocky progress of the journey—or rather, more often, the lack of it:

> Im nächtlichen Walde humpelt dahin
> Die Chaise. Da kracht es plötzlich—
> Ein Rad ging los. Wir halten still.
> Das ist nicht sehr ergötzlich. (canto 12; 1:463)

> (In the nocturnal forest the coach hobbles along.
> A sudden crash—
> A wheel got loose. We stop.
> That is not very amusing.)

At times, the "Chaise" seems mired in November mud:

> Ein feuchter Wind, ein kahles Land,
> Die Chaise wackelt im Schlamme;
> Doch singt es und klingt es in meinem Gemüt:
> "Sonne, du klagende Flamme!" (canto 14; 1:466)

> (A damp wind, a bleak land,
> The chaise wobbles in the mud,
> But in my mind there is a singing and ringing:
> Sun, you accusing [lamenting] flame!)

While the carriage bumps and limps across the bleak November landscape, the true activity takes place within the traveler's mind, as he reflects, dreams, and remembers. The people we encounter are, in the main, legendary and symbolic: Father Rhine, the three Magi, the Doppelgänger–lictor, Emperor Barbarossa, Hamburg's patroness Hammonia, and the young harpist whose "lullaby of heaven" greeted the traveler upon entering Germany.

The Barbarossa episode, which takes up four central cantos (14–17), shows the familiar mingling of nostalgia and satire, revealing Heine's peculiar conflict between emotional pulls and rational promptings, between the longings for a romantic retreat and considerations of the claims of the day.

The author's manner of introducing the legend deserves a closer look. After remarking on the bumpy ride, he withdraws into his revery ("doch singt es und klingt es in meinem Gemüt") by recalling two particularly memorable fairy-tales. Anyone who heard them in childhood will confirm the haunting quality of the story about the goose-girl and her faithful horse Falada, and of the archetypal tale of the murderer whose crime was revealed by the sun, "brought to light," as the tale's beautiful, poetic refrain reminds us: "Sonne, du klagende Flamme." It is all the more poignant when we recall the significance of the sun symbol for Heine. This refrain, interwoven into the gossamer web of fabled memories, gains import with every reprise. The mounting surge of nostalgia is now transferred to the Barbarossa myth, mentioned as the third of the echoing nursery tales. It is the legend of the great Kaiser Rotbart Barbarossa (Emperor Redbeard Barbarossa), asleep in Kyffhäuser Mountain, waiting for the day when he will liberate his beloved Germania and restore her to ancient glory.

This mythical aura is about to be dispelled as the traveling poet fantasizes about his visit at Kyffhäuser. He finds the Kaiser surrounded by his sleeping soldiers although he himself is not, as legend has it, seated, asleep, at the table, with his red beard growing through the stone, but up and about, doing his housekeeping chores: rubbing rust spots off some of the armor with his ermine-trimmed sleeve, brushing the peaked helmets with a duster of peacock feathers, and, since this happens to be the centennial payday, slipping a ducat into the pocket of each sleeping soldier. The time, he explains, is not yet ripe for his return. While his army is ready, his commissaries have been unable to supply him with the necessary complement of horses. "Why not use asses instead?" his visitor suggests, implying that there are plenty of them around. The Kaiser's queries about recent gossip are answered with an account that mainly chronicles beheadings of kings and nobles by means of a modern piece of machinery. Barbarossa is puzzled: What is a guillotine?

> "Du wirst hier an ein Brett geschnallt;—
> Das senkt sich;—du wirst geschoben
> Geschwinde zwischen zwei Pfosten;—es hängt
> Ein dreieckig Beil ganz oben;—
>
> Man zieht eine Schnur, dann schiesst herab
> Das Beil, ganz lustig und munter;—
> Bei dieser Gelegenheit fällt dein Kopf
> In einen Sack hinunter." (canto 16; 1:475)

> ("Here, they strap you onto a board;
> It comes down—you are quickly shoved
> Between two posts;
> Up there high, hangs a triangular hatchet;—
>
> They pull a cord, whereupon,
> Quite gaily and merrily, the hatchet shoots down;—
> At this occasion, your head
> drops [down] into a bag.")

The passage brings to mind Kafka's similarly dead-pan description of a torture machine[7] or certain passages in Günter Grass. Readers of Heine's lines will note the impact of the matter-of-fact account, with the speaker's gestures conveyed in the very wording; the cunning, insistent use of *du* when *man* would have served equally well, from a metric point of view, and would have been more idiomatic (and, under the circumstances, more diplomatic) together with the pairing, through the rhyme, of *munter* and *hinunter*. All of this achieves its subtle effect. The emperor rises to the bait, appalled—at the breach of etiquette!

"Der König und die Königin!
Geschnallt! an einem Brette!
Das ist ja gegen allen Respekt
Und alle Etikette!" (1:475)

("The king and the queen!
Buckled down! Onto a board!
But that runs counter to all respect
And all etiquette!")

This outburst awakens the visitor to the realization just how outdated old Redbeard actually is, and he returns him to the land of myth: go back to sleep, you old phantom, we shall liberate ourselves without you! With supreme irony, Heine had managed to distance himself from both, the old and the new way of doing things.

A highlight of *Wintermärchen* (Heine, by the way, was the first to use this short designation) is the traveler's arrival at his mother's house (canto 20). In two spare lines, with an exclamation and a gesture, the old lady virtually stands before us:

Und als ich zu meiner Frau Mutter kam,
Erschrak sie fast vor Freude;
Sie rief: "Mein liebes Kind!" und schlug
Zusammen die Hände beide. (1:483)

(And when I came to my mother
She was nearly stunned with joy;
She cried "my dear child!" and clasped
Her hands together.)

But typical mother that she was, she did not remain speechless for long. The next stanza hits exactly the right note:

"Mein liebes Kind, wohl dreizehn Jahr'
Verflossen unterdessen!
Du wirst gewiss sehr hungrig sein—
Sag an, was willst du essen?"

"My dear child, about thirteen years
Have meanwhile gone by!
You must be very hungry—
Tell me, what would you like to eat?"

The meal is accompanied by the motherly inquisition which includes some rather *verfängliche Fragen* ("captious questions"). What sort of a house does his wife run? Does she mend his socks and shirts?

"Der Fisch ist gut, lieb Mütterlein,
Doch muss man ihn schweigend verzehren;
Man kriegt so leicht eine Grät' in den Hals,
Du darfst mich jetzt nicht stören."

("The fish is good, dear mother,
But one must eat it in silence;
It is so easy to get a bone stuck in one's throat.
You must not disturb me now.")

The most ticklish query is reserved to the last:

"Mein liebes Kind! Wie denkst du jetzt?
Treibst du noch immer aus Neigung
Die Politik? Zu welcher Partei
Gehörst du mit Überzeugung?"

"Die Apfelsinen, lieb Mütterlein,
Sind gut, und mit wahrem Vergnügen
Verschlucke ich den süssen Saft,
Und ich lasse die Schalen liegen."

("My dear child! What is your thinking nowadays?
Are you still pursuing politics as a hobby?
To what party
Do you belong with conviction?")

"The oranges, dear mother,
Are good, and I swallow
Their sweet juice with real pleasure,
Leaving the peels aside.")

Note how the very act of evasion accentuates the import of the questions, how the replies at once conceal and reveal—while at the same time approximating an ordinary table conversation. And well might Mrs. Betty Heine have enquired about her son's political allegiances.

A day or so before his departure for Germany, Heine had made the acquaintance of Karl Marx, and for about eight months following his return—until Marx was expelled from France—the two men saw each other almost daily. Some scholars have recently focused attention on the nature and effect of this extraordinary meeting between the foremost German political satirist and the founder of modern communism, especially since the friendship with Marx also coincides with the most radical phase in Heine's writing.

It is well to keep in mind that, when he met Marx, Heine was forty-six years old and Marx's senior by twenty years. Heine was already a famous author with well-established and publicized opinions, including his views on communism. When speaking of "der Kommunismus" he did not mean an ideology but a specific movement which he had been watching for twelve years.[8] Nor did he apply the term—at least, not initially—to the men around Marx but to Babeuvism.[9] It goes without saying that this meeting of the minds must have had a stimulating, if not exhilarating, effect on both men. Heine was, moreover, affected in a practical way by the association with Marx and his associates (one of whom was the left Hegelian Arnold Ruge) inasmuch as it opened new outlets for his publications. As already mentioned, *Wintermärchen* was printed in *Vorwärts!* On the other hand, Marx demonstrates by numerous Heine quotations his intimate familiarity with (not to mention liking for) Heine's texts. And one famous phrase, usually attributed to Marx, about religion as "the opiate of the people," dulling the pains of a deprived mankind, was in fact borrowed from Heine's *Ludwig Börne* (6:194).

Understandably, the influence and stimulation was mutual, and it may not be altogether accidental that *Wintermärchen,* which originated during the peak of their friendship, is Heine's most provocative work. However, beyond his general empathy for the underdog and his concern for what he termed *die grosse Suppenfrage,* he showed little interest in economics, and certainly none in economic theory. Economic questions, far from seeming unimportant, were simply subsumed in the larger existential issue of the right to the good life.

In concluding the discussion of *Atta Troll. Ein Sommernachtstraum* and *Deutschland. Ein Wintermärchen,* an attempt to judge the two poems in conjunction seems to be in order, since their subtitles suggest that they are counterparts. They are, of course, quite independent of each other.

Yet related to each other by similarity as well as by contrast, they form a pair that is paradigmatic for Heine's divergent inclinations, his unsolved dilemma between opposite pulls. The contrasts are immediately apparent. While the one is Heine's politically most outspoken and radical poem, the other, on which he worked shortly before and after 1844, may be the most romantic and fantastic—which is neither to deny the nostalgic undercurrents of *Wintermärchen* nor the multitude of topical allusions that spice *Atta Troll*. Both mock epics consist of twenty-seven cantos made up of four-line stanzas, rhymed in one case, unrhymed in the other. Indeed, the flavor of *Atta Troll*'s elegant and urbane verse seems to have as much to do with the absence of rhyme as the exuberant thrust of *Wintermärchen* appears related to its obvious, and often eccentric and amusing, rhymes. There is also a fine, yet distinct, difference in the role and perspective of the narrator. In *Wintermärchen,* the narrator clearly speaks for the author at all times; in *Atta Troll,* the author's perspective is less obvious. Much of the time it is reflected in the persona of the hunter—a rather reluctant hunter, to be sure, who actually accompanies the real hunter Laskaro—who looks on the bear, as well as on the society which the bear harangues, with ironic detachment. Another, rather subtle contrast concerns the realism of the background. Whereas the political satire of *Wintermärchen,* with its account of a real journey, is expressed against and through a web of myth and legend, the backdrop of the fantastic tale is poignantly realistic!

Chapter Seven
The Later Poetry

In 1840, the *Augsburg Allgemeine Zeitung* reengaged Heine as its Paris correspondent. His commentaries on the cultural and political situation, subsequently published in the volume *Lutetia,* constitute an extraordinary achievement that has yet to be fully appreciated.[1] Covering an enormous range of topics, they give renewed evidence of Heine's varied interests, astute observation, and shrewd judgment. But, apart from these articles, he now returned to verse. It is as if writing *Ludwig Börne* had confirmed in him his self-understanding as primarily a poet. At the same time, the thematic breadth and scope of his poetry expanded to embrace the manifold concerns that had previously found expression mainly in his prose.

Second Pillar of Fame

Heine had never, of course, actually stopped writing verse, but now he prepared to gather it into another book. Published in 1844, *Neue Gedichte* [New Poems] shows his increasing sophistication, thematic versatility, and daring. It is divided into six parts. The opening cycle "Neuer Frühling" [New Spring] continues in the manner and mood of *Buch der Lieder*; the author's Saint-Simonian conviction and posture of confident sensualism is reflected, at times flaunted, in "Verschiedene" [Miscellaneous, or Variae]—the feminine adjective may be linked to "Gedichte" or taken as a wink in the direction of the Parisian grisettes whose names head most of the subgroups (without necessarily having much bearing on the poems in question). "Romanzen" [Romances] is the term Heine applies to the balladic narratives of love and adventure, a genre in which he continues to excel; "Zur Ollea" (from "Olla Podrida," a Spanish ragout) is what the name implies, a tasty mixture; "Zeitgedichte" [Poems of the Times] treat diverse topics of current interest. The epic "Deutschland. Ein Wintermärchen" [Germany, a Winter's Tale] concludes the volume.

One of these poems has deservedly become a folksong:

> Leise zieht durch mein Gemüt
> Liebliches Geläute.
> Klinge, kleines Frühlingslied,
> Kling hinaus ins Weite.
>
> Kling hinaus, bis an das Haus,
> Wo die Blumen spriessen.
> Wenn du eine Rose schaust,
> Sag, ich lass sie grüssen. (1:217–18)
>
> (Softly passes through my heart
> A sweet, bell-like tune.
> Ring forth, little song of spring
> Ring forth into the distance.
>
> Ring forth toward the house
> Where the flowers blossom,
> When you see a rose around
> Say I send her greetings.)

It is a song about a song, sent forth as a messenger to the beloved. Unparalleled in its sparseness—the only trope is the oblique allusion to the "one and only" rose among the flowers—it weaves its ephemeral spell through melodious, onomatopoetic sounds and rhythms, echoing the bell effect of "liebliches Geläute" in the first stanza while evoking opening vistas in the second.

Love is still a major theme, the mood is still melancholy. But the plaint is less about unrequited love than about love's (and life's) transitoriness:

> Es ragt ins Meer der Runenstein,
> Da sitz ich mit meinen Träumen.
> Es pfeift der Wind, die Möwen schrein,
> Die Wellen, die wandern und schäumen.

Ich habe geliebt manch schönes Kind
Und manchen guten Gesellen—
Wo sind sie hin? Es pfeift der Wind,
Es schäumen und wandern die Wellen. (1:241)

(The rune stone juts into the sea,
I sit there with my dreams.
There whistles the wind, the seagulls screech,
The waves they wander and foam.

I have loved many a beautiful girl
And many a good lad—
Where are they now? There whistles the wind,
The waves roll on, foaming and wandering.)

The effect of the mood-picture derives from the contrast between the primordial quality and permanence of the setting and the sense of frailty and transience felt by the meditating self. "Es ragt ins Meer der Runenstein": A lapidary sentence in which meaning and sound are inseparably fused conjures up the rune stone, epitome of immutability and ancient mystery, and the sea, ageless and unfathomable. "Da sitz ich mit meinen Träumen": simple fact, stated in a prosaic way which, in its contrast to the majestic force of the first line, makes the "ich" seem insignificant and his fantasies ephemeral. Presently the stark and static scene seems enveloped in movement: the whistling wind, the screeching gulls, the foaming, rolling surf, all signify fleeting motion. And again we return to the uncertain, questioning "I": "Wo sind sie hin?" Where has love and life gone? There follows, as a response of sorts, a reiteration of the preceding two lines, with a subtle inversion—just enough variation to suggest the circularity, infinity of time and the perpetual motion of an indifferent nature. Heine has a special talent for exploiting a refrain in a way which heightens its emotional charge with each successive repetition.

Another such shift and intensification from one refrain to the next occurs in a poem which also exemplifies the extension of the love theme. It is a lament about homesickness, written not long after Heine moved to Paris:

Ich hatte einst ein schönes Vaterland.
Der Eichenbaum

Wuchs dort so hoch, die Veilchen nickten sanft.
Es war ein Traum.

Das küsste mich auf deutsch, und sprach auf deutsch
(Man glaubt es kaum,
Wie gut es klang) das Wort: "Ich liebe dich!"
Es war ein Traum. (1:279)

(I once had a German fatherland.
The oaktree
Grew there so tall, the violets gently nodded.
It was a dream.

In German, I felt a kiss, and heard the words
[Hard to believe,
How good they sounded]: "I love you!"
It was a dream.)

Note the peculiar effect of the alternating long and short lines: the pentameters tell the tale, while the dimeters carry the rhyme and the emphasis, with greatest weight on the refrain. The first stanza of this variation on the theme of unrequited love is made up entirely of clichés, including the one that reveals the tall oaks and gently nodding violets to be figments of fantasy; but the same denouement acquires a strange poignancy when it occurs a second time, showing the poet's wishful notion, that his fatherland lovingly accepts him, to be an idle dream. Somehow, between the first stanza and the second, a subtle shift in the meaning of *Traum* has taken place. In the first instance, "dream" carries the (positive) emotional charge of its romantic, albeit clichéd, connotation; in the second instance, its more negative sense, with emphasis on deception and disappointment is evoked.

The distinction between sensitivity and sentimentality is not easily drawn, and many Heine poems hover precariously on the borderline. Some pieces profoundly affect one reader and seem maudlin to another. As we have already seen, Heine himself was quick to mock hollow emotionalism. He does so in this well-known ditty:

Das Fräulein stand am Meere
Und seufzte lang und bang,
Es rührte sie so sehre
Der Sonnenuntergang.

"Mein Fräulein! sein Sie munter,
Das ist ein altes Stück;
Hier vorne geht sie unter
Und kehrt von hinten zurück." (1:240)

(The miss stood by the ocean
Heaving long and anguished sighs,
She was stirred so very greatly
By the setting sun.

"Cheer up, young lady,
This is an old number;
Here in front it goes down
And comes back from behind.")

The parody speaks for itself. However, at the risk of spoiling the joke, one might ask by what means Heine achieves the desired comic effect. To begin with, his rhetoric shows the lady's exhibition of sentiment to be excessive ("und seufzte lang und bang") and affected ("es rührte sie so sehre"—"sehre" being an archaic, stilted form, here, moreover, seemingly reclaimed for the sake of the rhyme). This exaggerated display is debunked by the opposite attitude: a voice, presumably male, so crassly sober-sided that it is equally extreme. Nor is it a coincidence that it is a spinster who displays this sentimentality: in Heine's view, the capacity for authentic emotional experience is reserved for the male.

"Seraphine" et al.

The two last cited poems belong to the more innocuous items in the cycle "Verschiedene" which in its time caused a considerable raising of eyebrows. Starting with groups entitled—obviously tongue-in-cheek—"Seraphine" and "Angelique," it continues with a veritable Leporello list of supposed conquests: "Diana," "Hortense," "Clarisse," "Yolante," "Marie," "Emma," "Friedrike," and "Katherina."[2] The bulk of these poems, the first Heine composed in France, date back to the early 1830s when he, too, was in his thirties and in the full flush of health and good fortune. The historical essays that originated concurrently show sensualism to be on the verge of victory over spiritualism, or rather, on the verge of achieving a synthesis with spiritualism. But in these verses the struggle appears to be over, the dualism overcome, body and soul in harmony and of equal dignity. At least so the poet would have us believe. Pantheism, the Saint-Simonian message, and his personal sense of well-being and vigor, as well as access to the Parisian cornucopia of metropolitan offerings, combine to inspire his exultant praise of sensuality.

To Heine's compatriots, these frankly erotic poems, which first appeared in print in 1833 and 1834,[3] seemed very risqué. Even Karl Gutzkow, whose own novel *Wally die Zweiflerin* [Wally the Skeptic] had triggered the decree of censorship in 1835 and landed its author in jail, warned Heine in 1838 against reprinting these "immoral" poems. Feigning polite gratitude to Gutzkow for having pointed out "this mote in my eye," Heine countered with a reference to such acknowledged masterpieces as the *Satiricon* by Petronius and Goethe's *Römische Elegien* [Roman Elegies]: should one hesitate to have them reprinted as well? Like them, Heine continues, "my own controversial (*angefochtene*) poems are no food for the broad masses (*robe Massen*)."[4] He clearly felt himself in advance of his time, and history has proved him right: to modern sensibilities the poems grouped under the heading "Verschiedene" seem relatively tame.

Most celebrated among them is "Seraphine" No. 7. It succinctly encompasses Heine's "new creed" of pantheistic sensualism:

Auf diesem Felsen bauen wir
Die Kirche von dem dritten,
Dem dritten neuen Testament;
Das Leid ist ausgelitten.

Vernichtet ist das Zweierlei,
Das uns so lang betöret;
Die dumme Leiberquälerei
Hat endlich aufgehöret.

Hörst du den Gott im finstern Meer?
Mit tausend Stimmen spricht er.
Und siehst du über unserm Haupt
Die tausend Gotteslichter?

Der heil'ge Gott, der ist im Licht
Wie in den Finsternissen;
Und Gott ist alles, was da ist;
Er ist in unsern Küssen. (1:238; "Seraphine," No. 7)

(Upon this rock we build
The church of the third,
The third New Testament.
All suffering is over.

The dualism is destroyed
Which had so long deluded us;
The stupid torment of the flesh
Has finally been ended.

Do you hear God's voice in the dark sea?
He speaks with thousand voices.
And do you see above our head
The thousand divine lights?

The holy God is in the light
As in the darkness(es);
And God is everything there is;
He is in our kisses.)

The utopian vision of a third New Testament goes back to the twelfth-century theologian Joachim de Fiore. However, the new gospel proclaimed by Heine is of an entirely different kind than the Calabrian monk, who had founded a monastery on rigidly ascetic principles, had in mind. It is precisely Heine's opposition to Christian tenets—indeed, his reversal of traditional values—which makes for the ironic force of a stanza that begins with God's all-pervading presence in light and darkness—echoing Genesis—only to team "Finsternisse" with "Küsse" in the punch line. A harmonious balance between the demands of body and mind, Heine maintains, produces a natural morality while the repression of sensuality—and Heine means beauty as well as sex—is harmful and fundamentally immoral.

What makes this poem quintessentially Heinesque—and must have compounded its heretical impact on his contemporaries who read it in the context of the cycle—is its piquant ambivalence.[5] For "Seraphine,"

No. 7 contains not only a graphic summary of Heine's creed but also, quite literally, the climactic moment in an amorous chase which had been the topic of the two or three preceding poems. There, the lover had been in hot pursuit of the nimble-footed "Seraphine," along the rocks, overlooking the sea, against the setting sun; finally catching up with her "Auf diesem Felsen." The "du" and "wir" with which, we feel, he is addressing the benevolent reader or universal fellowman, actually means an intimate partner.

Bridging the Gulf

One of the many paradoxes about Heine is that it took him so long to overcome the rather artificial segregation of topics suitable for prose and for poetry: although he had, almost from the beginning of his career, called for a literature responsive to the concerns of the age, he had confined his critical comment on the body politic to his prose while seemingly unable to free his verse from the domination of the love theme.[6] The interlude of the *Nordsee* poems, where he managed to break away from the folksong pattern, had, despite the success of these free verses, remained just that, an interlude, after which he returned to the four-line stanza and idiom of the *Buch der Lieder*. He greatly admired Walther von der Vogelweide; but he paid no heed to the fact that this Minnesinger was also a political poet. Even more baffling is his distance from the German political poets of his own era, authors such as Georg Herwegh, Hoffmann von Fallersleben, Ferdinand Freiligrath, whom, one should expect, he might have regarded as kindred spirits. Instead, he mocked what he called their *Tendenzpoesie* ("tendentious poetry") at every opportunity, most notably in his epic *Atta Troll*.

To be sure, even while he had maintained the division between politically relevant prose and supposedly more exalted poetry that dealt with the private sphere or with romantic fantasies, certain realistic touches and sociopolitical asides had gradually crept in. But it had been an incidental and almost inadvertent invasion. (The transitional function of the "Tannhäuser" poem has already been pointed out.) Now, for whatever reason—the catharsis achieved by writing the Börne book has already been mentioned—a conscious and deliberate breakthrough occurred, signaled by the title of the last group of *Neue Gedichte*: "Zeitgedichte." Nor is this a passing interlude. Henceforth, political and social actualities will be a proper subject for poesy as well, and there will be no more separation between the public and the private domaine in Heine's work. Indeed, the constant and sometimes startling interplay of personal and general implications will add a singular flavor to his late poetry. Moreover, given Heine's flair for controlling perspectives and his skill of adapting poetic expression to the topic, so that the medium becomes the message, this thematic expansion opens up infinite possibilities of enrichment in tone and voice. But most important, and most welcome of all, are the added opportunities for the display of Heine's sparkling humor and the cutting edge of his wit.

At the head of "Zeitgedichte" stands the poem entitled "Doktrin" [Doctrine] where the author introduces the new role he envisages for himself: that of the drummer who arouses the apathetic sleepers. This is the opening stanza:

> Schlage die Trommel und fürchte dich nicht,
> Und küsse die Marketenderin!
> Das ist die ganze Wissenschaft,
> Das ist der Bücher tiefster Sinn. (1:319)

> (Beat the drum and do not be afraid
> And kiss the canteen woman!
> That is the sum total of all philosophy,
> That is the profoundest meaning of the books.)

The sound of the drum dictates the poem's beat, repeated and reinforced in the next stanza. And finally:

> Das ist die Hegelsche Philosophie,
> Das ist der Bücher tiefster Sinn!
> Ich hab sie begriffen, weil ich gescheit,
> Und weil ich ein guter Tambour bin.

> (That is the Hegelian philosophy,
> That is the profoundest meaning of the books!
> I understand it because I am smart
> And because I am a good drummer.)

Nowadays Heine is, in fact, acknowledged to have been among the first who recognized the radical implications of Hegel's thought. As for the boldness of the Tambour's concluding assertion: buried in the self-confident boast is an oblique message. His understanding of Hegel's fundamental import is not merely based on his intellectual faculty (although this is a sine qua non, to be sure!) but on the particular sensitivity that goes with being a "good drummer." The drummer is a transparent mask for the poet who, according to Heine, is endowed with special insight almost by definition. The grand claim serves to characterize his naive dash; yet the ultimate line introduces, ever so subtly, a touch of irony when the drummer's forceful and regular beat seems to have difficulty coping with "guter Tambour" without wrenching the accent.

Following immediately in the sequence of the cycle—and we know that Heine arranged the order of his poems with great care—is a piece that turns out to be of similarly telling, one almost wants to say programmatic, significance. Entitled "Adam der Erste" [Adam the First], it shows Adam protesting the expulsion from paradise. Here are the first four stanzas (out of six):

Du schicktest mit dem Flammenschwert
Den himmlischen Gendarmen,
Und jagtest mich aus dem Paradies,
Ganz ohne Recht und Erbarmen!

Ich ziehe fort mit meiner Frau
Nach andren Erdenländern;
Doch dass ich genossen des Wissens Frucht,
Das kannst du nicht mehr ändern.

Du kannst nicht ändern, dass ich weiss,
Wie sehr du klein und nichtig,
Und machst du dich auch noch so sehr
Durch Tod und Donnern wichtig.

O Gott! wie erbärmlich ist doch dies
Consilium abeundi!
Das nenne ich einen Magnifikus
Der Welt, ein lumen mundi! (1:319–20)

(You have sent the heavenly gendarme
With the flaming sword
And chased me from paradise,

Unfairly and mercilessly!

I move on, with my wife,
To other lands;
But that I have tasted the fruit of knowledge,
This you can no longer change.

Nor can you change (the fact) that I know
How small and insignificant you are,
No matter how you throw your weight around
With death and thunder.

Oh God! how pitiable is this
Consilium abeundi!
And that is supposed to be a Magnificus
Of the world, a lumen mundi!)

We are struck first of all by the expressiveness of the rhythm leading up to the expletive force with which, in stanza four, the defiance of that almighty "Du," with which the poem began, is uttered. Adam, as the title implies, is but the first of all the victimized Adams, down to the author whose consilium abeundi from Göttingen University supplies a clever analogy, making profound and trivial, general and private meanings merge: while Jehovah similarly merges with the rector (Magnificus), the censor, and all arbitrary authority. As for the comic effect of Adam's reference to the archangel as a "heavenly gendarme," to Eve as "my wife," or to Jehovah as a pompous tyrant full of self-importance, it is one of Heine's specialties to present sublime subjects from the perspective of commonplace experience, invariably with humorous but also illuminating effect.

Many "Zeitgedichte" are virtually untranslatable, at least without a great deal of explanation. They must have been all the more intriguing and funny for contemporaries who got the point without the benefit of footnotes. The central figure of the poem "Der Kaiser von China" [The Emperor of China], for example, could be readily identified as Frederick William IV.

Here are stanzas one, seven, and eight (out of a total of ten):

Mein Vater war ein trockner Taps,
Ein nüchterner Duckmäuser,
Ich aber trinke meinen Schnaps
Und bin ein grosser Kaiser.

Die grosse Pagode, Symbol und Hort
Des Glaubens, ist fertig geworden;
Die letzten Juden taufen sich dort
Und kriegen den Drachenorden

Es schwindet der Geist der Revolution,
Und es rufen die edelsten Mandschu:
"Wir wollen keine Konstitution,
Wir wollen den Stock, den Kantschu!" (1:333–34)

(My father was a dry lout
A sober milk-toast,
But I drink my Schnaps
And am a great emperor.

The great pagoda, symbol and treasury
Of faith, has been completed;
The last Jews are being baptized there
And get the Dragon order.

The spirit of the Revolution is disappearing
And the noblest Manschu exclaim:
"We want no constitution,
We want the cane, the Kantschu [leather whip]!)

Of course the "great pagoda" is easily recognized as Cologne cathedral, the Order of the Dragon as the "Schwanenorden" (Order of the Swan, a medieval order which Frederick William attempted to revive in 1843), and elsewhere in the poem, Confusius as Schelling. It may not be great poetry but as satire it was deadly.

No explanatory note is required for the last poem in the group:

Denk ich an Deutschland in der Nacht,
Dann bin ich um den Schlaf gebracht,

Ich kann nicht mehr die Augen schliessen,
Und meine heissen Tränen fliessen.

Die Jahre kommen und vergehn!
Seit ich die Mutter nicht gesehn,
Zwölf Jahre sind schon hingegangen;
Es wächst mein Sehnen und Verlangen. (1:339)

(When I think of Germany at night,
I am robbed of my sleep,
I can no longer close my eyes
And my hot tears are flowing.

The years come and go!
Since I saw my mother last
Twelve years have passed;
My longing and my yearning grows.)

These are the first two stanzas of "Nachtgedanken" [Night Thoughts]. Their opening lines have been frequently cited to express the ambivalent, disturbing, intensely personal patriotism of the exile. The poet—and the voice here is clearly Heine's own—is wretched with longing for his mother whom he has not seen for twelve years. Throughout the ten stanzas, he keeps reverting to the same lament, the passing of the years, the ever-growing pain of separation, the fear that the old woman may die: "Das Vaterland wird nie verderben, / Jedoch die alte Frau kann sterben" ("The fatherland will never perish / but the old woman may die"). It is a tear-jerking litany of clichés, from the flood of hot tears and the longing and yearning to the oaks and linden, perennial emblems of Germany's sturdiness. The meter—rhymed pairs with alternating male and female endings that make for melancholy, even cadences—also seems all too smooth and predictable. Yet the poem is strangely memorable. A nightmarish spell results from the insistent reverberation of the same nagging thoughts. Again and again, an earlier line, perhaps slightly modified, comes back, creating the impression of gnawing worry, of the grip of incubus, of sleepless tossing. Minutes seem to be standing still while we bemoan the years that have slipped by. In the end, the torment mounts unbearably as the poet, obsessively counting the dead bodies of those who have died while he has lived in exile, feels smothered by their weight. The dream ends as dreams do:

Gottlob! durch meine Fenster bricht
Französisch heitres Tageslicht;
Es kommt mein Weib, schön wie der Morgen,
Und lächelt fort die deutschen Sorgen.

(Thank God! through my window breaks
Serene French sunlight;
My wife arrives, beautiful as the morning,
And smiles away the German sorrows.)

The contrast of mood is conveyed with seemingly artless simplicity, making the relief of awakening as real as the nightmare had been. Does not the rhyme with "schön wie der Morgen" practically lift the weight off "Sorgen"?

The Mattress Grave

The year in which Heine journeyed home, produced *Deutschland: Ein Wintermärchen,* brought out *Neue Gedichte,* and met Karl Marx was eventful in yet another way. Uncle Salomon died. But instead of the lifetime pension which the nephew believed to have been promised— which, together with a subsidy granted him by the French government, would have given him reasonable financial security—he received only a modest legacy. Salomon Heine's main heir, his son Carl, was willing to continue his cousin's pension only on condition that he publish nothing about the family. What was at stake were the mysterious memoirs to which the author had alluded from time to time. Heine was very upset.[7] He felt betrayed by the family, treated worse than by the Prussian censor. But Carl eventually won out, the memoirs—if they ever existed—were (supposedly) destroyed and the pension was continued. But it was a long and unpleasant feud. Reflected in Heine's correspondence, the inheritance dispute makes very painful reading, showing him desperately engaged in all kind of unsavory stratagems to force his family into acknowledging his entitlement. The stresses and strains of the quarrel are believed to have contributed to the poet's physical breakdown.

Heine's constitution had never been robust. After enjoying a relatively healthy interlude in his thirties when he was described—by himself as much as by others—as downright corpulent, disquieting signals of impending trouble became ever more frequent till, in his fiftieth year, his health broke down completely. After May, 1848, he never walked again. The cause of the disease that was to entomb him in his *Matratzengruft* ("mattress grave") for eight years is now assumed to have been a venereal infection that settled in his spinal cord. His accounts of his discomforts, mostly in letters to friends and family— although he took great care to keep the grim details from his mother— are heartrending. Not only were his legs and at times his right arm paralyzed but he also suffered from excruciating abdominal cramps that forced him to lie curled up on his side for days on end. Blind in one eye, he could use the other only when he held up the eyelid with his fingers. For a time he had also lost his sense of taste and his paralyzed jaw made speech difficult.

The recital of these distressing details is necessary to bring into focus the manner in which he bore up and responded to his suffering. Incredible as it may seem, he did not lose his reverence for life nor did he turn into an embittered world-hater. Beside the opium which was administered in ever more massive doses, his foremost anodyne was poetry. Almost miraculously, he remained lucid, productive, and in charge of his brilliant wit practically to his last hour. His sense of humor and his poetic powers helped him to surmount the torment and the terror and to transform his personal plight into a generally accessible experience: "Aus meinen grossen Schmerzen mach ich die kleinen Lieder" ("Out of my great pains I make my little songs"), he had said when he was a love-sick young poet (1:86). If the genuineness of those "great pains" has, perhaps justly, occasionally been called in question, there can be no doubt about the authenticity of the experience out of which he created his late poems. If the sudden shifts and reversals of mood in his earlier verse have appeared to some readers to be but a frivolous, seemingly facile game, his mocking tone and ironic distance now imparts dignity, attests to the resilience and dominant radiance of a human mind in the face of unspeakable misery. The poetry that so tellingly conveys Heine's encounter with pain and death is not only considered by many to be his finest achievement but it includes passages that belong to the most moving in German literature.

By strange coincidence, the year of Heine's physical collapse was also the year of political unrest which brought to an end the regime of the "Citizen-King" Louis-Philippe whose ascension to the throne the poet had exuberantly celebrated as a sign that sociopolitical progress was possible. Like the July Revolution eighteen years earlier, the February rebellion of 1848 took three days to unseat a monarch. But there the parallel ends. In the following three months, the battlelines were grimly drawn between the socialist and conservative elements, culminating in the bloody June days when ten thousand persons were killed and wounded and as many more thrown into prison. The new government was first headed by the poet Lamartine and subsequently by Louis Napoleon Bonaparte, who declared himself Napoleon III, suppressing the socialist opposition, and establishing a dictatorship "more demagogic, more calculating, more hollow, and more modern than any that the first Napoleon had ever imagined."[8]

Although Heine had foreseen and foretold the end of the July monarchy, he took no satisfaction from this event. At first sympathetic to the regime of Lamartine, he soon changed his mind, just as he was to be disillusioned about Louis Napoleon, whom he had initially welcomed. Nor was he pleased by the German revolution of 1848 which, he feared, would not so much produce democratic reform as reinforce nationalist tendencies. As it turned out, his prophecy proved accurate in the long run. As he said in a letter to Gustav Kolb, the liberal-minded editor of the *Augsburg Allgemeine Zeitung*: "The beautiful ideals of political morality, legality, civic virtue, freedom and equality, the rosy-dawn dreams of the eighteenth century for which our fathers so heroically marched to death and which we no less heroically dreamed after them—there they lie at our feet, trodden down, scattered, like the shards of a porcelain bowl."[9]

These lines were written in retrospect. But Heine had expressed his ambivalence even in the midst of the upheaval, as in this letter to Alfred Meissner: "You can easily understand my feelings at the revolution which I saw taking place before my very eyes. As you know, I was no republican. . . . You will not be surprised that I was terribly moved for a moment and cold shivers ran down my spine. . . . Well, it has passed. . . . Gladly would I flee the turmoil of public life that so oppresses me, to the immortal spring of poetry . . . if only I could walk better and were not ill."[10]

This was written a month before his legs gave out completely and turned, as he put it, "into cottonwool." Illness, political disillusion, breach with Campe[11]—but there was still more trouble in store. Following the revolution, the fact that he had been receiving a government pension (a fact that he had freely discussed with his friends) was made public. Not only was he more in need of financial support than ever before—the stipend had been ordered stopped by Lamartine—but the disclosure put him under an intolerable cloud of suspicion. Then and thereafter, his detractors did not cease to denounce him as a traitor, although no one could say just what he is supposed to have betrayed or to whom. There is no evidence that he rendered any service in return for his pension. His critique of French politics had been uncompromisingly outspoken, so much so that his assignment as a correspondent for the *Augsburg Allgemeine Zeitung* had been discontinued because he was too liberal. Nevertheless even the *Allgemeine Zeitung* insinuated that he was paid by the French not for what he wrote but for what he did not write. Fiercely proud of his independence which had earned him attacks from the right and from the left, Heine was so embarrassed and upset by these allegations that he offered a public explanation, defending the pension as a generous act of the French government in aid of an exile from an oppressive regime, intended to compensate him for the loss of income incurred by the federal ban of 1835. He vigorously denied ever having in any sense been bought (7:351).

This explanation was not the only public declaration with regard to his personal affairs and conduct that the poet felt called upon to publish during a career which, more than that of any other author before or possibly since, has unfolded before the public eye and has engaged public interest and controversy. What other writer could have issued a *Berichtigung* ("correction") such as appeared in the *Augsburg Allgemeine Zeitung* on April 25, 1849, regarding the allowance he now received from his family, and announcing the transformation that had taken place within him since his confinement to the sickbed: "I am no longer a divine biped, I am no longer the freest German since Goethe. . . . I am no longer the Great Pagan No. 2. . . . I am now only a poor mortally sick Jew, an emaciated picture of misery, an unhappy man" (7:354).

Thus Heine adverted publicly to what has been called his "return to God," a dramatic reversal by one who had proclaimed the death of God in all manner of formulations. This change of mind puzzled his contemporaries as well as later biographers and interpreters.[12] Did he really mean to cancel out everything he had written and stood for? Was it the vision of truth in the face of death or the aberration of a sick mind, to be discounted? Was it a last gigantic hoax by one who had always liked to mystify people?[13] Or had he, as some will have it, always been a "baroque believer"? Throughout his life Heine had addressed God as an ever-present witness and companion. Never interested in theological argument or ontological proof, he admitted to a profound sense of awe before the miracle of life, of human reason, of love and beauty, and he felt that his own creativity was part of some higher force.[14] So what did he mean when he proclaimed, again and again, the death of God?

He had of course simply meant the death of belief in a god figure who takes personal charge of human affairs; and he meant the unhealthy preoccupation with and reliance on otherworldly promises while downgrading human happiness and fulfillment on earth; he meant institutionalized religion and doctrine—what he termed "positive religion" in contrast to a natural feeling of religiosity—which he viewed as an impediment, psychologically as well as in sociopolitical development. (In his refusal to have any part of church or synagogue he never faltered, and he stipulated in his will that no clergy of any denomination was to take part in his funeral.)

Personal and political progress is dependent on emancipation from the bonds of orthodoxy, so he thought when he was healthy and confidently convinced that human progress was unlimited and inevitable, with promise for an abundant life for all. And he viewed the Christian religion as an invention founded to console the poor and the disinherited: "Für Menschen, denen die Erde nichts mehr bietet, ward der Himmel erfunden . . . geistiges Opium, einige Tropfen Liebe, Hoffnung, Glauben!" ("Heaven was invented for those to whom earth has nothing more to offer . . . spiritual opiate, a few drops of love, hope, faith! 6:194). This is the crux: Heaven was invented by man. Religion is without transcendental validity, a psychological phenomenon judged entirely by its effect on the human condition. But whereas in his prime Heine had thought it had a negative, impeding effect, changed circumstances forced him to change his mind. He stressed repeatedly that there was no overwhelming emotional experience involved in his "return," no revelation "on the road to Damascus," but that it was a conscious intellectual decision, a rational change of opinion.

The stories that are circulating about my present religiosity and piety ["Frömmelei"] have been mixed with much nonsense and even more malice.

There has not been such a great change in my religious feeling, and the only inner event of which I can report with definite assurance consists in the fact that a February Revolution has also occurred in my religious views and thoughts; and I have replaced an earlier concept . . . with a new one. . . . With one word, I have given up the Hegelian God, or rather the Hegelian godlessness, and in its place I have again pulled out [*wieder hervorgezogen*] the dogma of a real, personal God who is outside nature and apart from the human mind. . . . Hegel has sunk very low in my estimation, and old Moses is in the ascendancy. If only I had his prophets along with Moses! ["To have Moses and his prophets": a student expression for being solvent.][15]

Yes, it is indeed the description of the traditional, personal old God, but, of course, the key word is the verb: "habe . . . wieder hervorgezogen." He pulled out the concept of God consciously and deliberately, as one retrieves an old file.

The most memorable of Heine's references to his "return" is the account of his last outing. Factual or invented, the tale gloriously exemplifies his genius for metaphoric condensation. In May, 1848, he left his house for the last time to visit the Louvre. There he broke down, before, of all places, the Venus of Milo, "die hochgebenedeite Göttin der Schönheit, Unsere liebe Frau von Milo" ("The blessed Goddess of Beauty, Our dear Lady of Milo," 2:190); "Zu ihren Füssen lag ich lange, und ich weinte so heftig, dass sich dessen ein Stein erbarmen musste. Auch schaute die Göttin mitleidig auf mich herab, doch zugleich so trostlos, als wollte sie sagen: siehst du nicht, dass ich keine Arme habe und also nicht helfen kann?" ("I lay at her feet for a long time and I wept so violently that even a stone had to be moved to pity. And the Goddess looked down on me compassionately yet also disconsolately, as if to say: How can I help you? Don't you see that I have no arms?"). The episode is from the postscript to *Romanzero* where he makes a public recantation of his atheism, and it sets the tone: his sense of irony is intact. It also prepares the scene: he needs a God that can help.

To have a will, one must be a person, and to exercise it, one needs to have one's elbows free. So when we desire a God who is able to help—and that is, after all, the main thing—we must also assume his personality, his metaphysical existence, and his holy attributes: goodness, omniscience, justice, etc. The immortality of the soul, our survival beyond death, is then added as a bonus like the beautiful soup bone which the butcher slips gratis into the basket of his good customers." (2:188)

All of Heine's utterances about his "return" have this in common that he continues to consider Jehovah to be a figment of man's imagination. The only thing that has changed is his opinion as to his—or society's—need for the belief in "this old superstition." Heine referred to his "transformation" as a "February Revolution." The events of 1848 had filled him with dismay in more ways than one. Religious emancipation was to have been a step toward achieving a better kind of humanity, and to have prepared the way for a just society and a world of beauty. Instead, he sees atheism proclaimed by what he calls *rohe Plebs* ("plebeian riff-raff"): atheism did not free people—on the contrary. He sees ideologists as slaves of fixed ideas "We now have monks of atheism. . . . I must confess, I do not like this music" (7:306). And while he used to decry the bond between feudal interests and religion, he now fears another alliance even more: "ein mehr oder minder geheimes Bündnis . . . mit dem schauderhaft nacktesten, ganz feigenblattlosen, kommunen Kommunismus" ("a more or less secret alliance with the most horribly naked, undisguised" ˙ [literally, "figleaf-less"], communal communism," 7:129). He is now convinced that the world, as well as he personally, cannot dispense with a belief in God.

The most pervasive, and in a sense the most persuasive constant in his religious attitude(s) is the poet's ironic tone of voice, even when, or better: especially when he addresses his newly acknowledged God of old. Indeed, it is as if he mainly needed him as an addressee for his pungent, scathing witticisms. Not surprisingly, it is this fact which critics who look on Heine's "theological revision" from a Christian point of view have found most perplexing. For whatever he may have asserted about the return of the "prodigal son" (2:188) to his "personal, omnipotent, transcendent" father, he speaks to him with the same mocking and defiant irreverence that had always been his trademark. He threatens to report the "great tormentor of animals" (*Tierquäler*) to the Society for the Prevention of Cruelty to Animals—then as now, "inhumane" treatment of animals constituted a particularly heinous crime—and he reminds him what genial, good-natured God he, Heine, had been when he achieved divine status "by the grace of Hegel." He expresses relief at no longer having to spend money on charity, now that he has joined the ranks of the pious and can leave the matter in God's hands; and he reminds him on this occasion that it takes a deity with much money and good health to run the world. He points out to the "heavenly Aristophanes," who enjoys his jest with his little colleague, that this comedy has a flaw: it has been protracted far too long. As a parting shot, he is reported to have quipped, in reply to the question whether he made his peace with God: "dieu me pardonnera—c'est son métier" ("God will forgive me—that's his job").

While he perpetually contrasts a happier past with the bleak present, dwelling with particular irony on the defeat of the proud "Hellene," there is no hint anywhere of a sense of guilt or a suggestion that his plight might constitute punishment for his hubris. On the contrary; he chides God for his inconsistency:

> Ob deiner Inkonsequenz, o Herr,
> Erlaube, dass ich staune:
> Du schufest den fröhlichsten Dichter, und raubst
> Ihm jetzt seine gute Laune. (2:432)

> (Your inconsistency, oh lord—
> Permit my saying so—astounds me:
> You created the gayest of poets, and now
> You rob him of his good humor.)

To sum up, now that the poet is more than ever an outsider, doomed to the ultimate loneliness of the moribund, isolated from the world of ordinary people by that unbridgeable chasm, the wretched business of dying ("le vilain métier de moribond")[16] he seeks in God a partner in colloquy, to whom to pour out his complaint and protest. He does not take back his celebration of life nor retract his call for the abolition of the self-destructive sense of guilt. His very tone, the vigor, ingenuity, and color, in short, the undiminished poetic beauty of the verse that he continues to produce, as well as the humor which permeates his written work and conversations, represents, if not victory, an abiding testimonial to the sturdiness and dignity of the human spirit.

Romanzero, and after

The poetic oeuvre produced by Heine on his death bed is not only impressive for its sophistication and virtuosity but also astounding in its dimensions. In Kaufmann's edition, the poems composed after 1848 fill sixty pages. Apart from those that Heine himself still submitted to the publisher, namely, *Romanzero* and *Gedichte* (1853–54)—the latter in *Vermischte Schriften* [Miscellaneous Writings] where they separated *Geständnisse* [Confessions] from miscellaneous other prose—a substantial number were first published posthumously.

Karl Hillebrand, who served for a time as Heine's secretary, recorded how the poet in his sleepless nights would compose some of his most beautiful poems: "He dictated the whole of the *Romanzero* to me. Every poem was quite complete in the morning."[17] But there then began a painstaking process of revision, determining the precise word and perfect cadence. Contemporary reports such as Hillebrand's and comparisons[18] of variant versions of poems, where they exist, make us appreciate how Heine's poetic intuition and imagination was complemented by meticulous attention to detail, a craftsman's skill, and a sensitive ear for nuances. Expressions were tightened, unnecessary adjectives dropped, more vivid images found. Sometimes a seemingly minute change made all the difference. Phrases that seemed too mannered, too crude, or too personal were frequently eliminated. But of special importance were rhythmic and tonal subtleties, the timbre of dark or light vowels, the quality of soft or harsh consonants, and the effect of the interplay between sound and meaning, so that images were reinforced by the sounds and rhythms of language itself. In contrast to his early poetry where tonal cadences ("that typical Heine melody") often prevailed independent of meaning, the later work shows an increasing regard for the meaningful synergism of grammar and meter: the prosody helps a certain word or phrase to stand out, metrical stress is made to support key words. "I have worked, really worked at my poems,"[19] Heine remarked, and one tends to believe him, wondering which is more remarkable, the astonishing act of creation or the meticulous revision, given the circumstances.

When Heine proposed the publication of a new book of poetry which he hoped would complement the other two as the "third pillar of (his) lyrical fame,"[20] Campe finally ended the three years of sulking during which he had not answered Heine's letters, and traveled to Paris to negotiate the new project. To call it "Romanzero" was his idea.

The title actually applies mainly to the first of the book's three sections: "Historien" [Histories]. Here the poet externalizes his experience in balladic narratives that take us into distant times and places, beginning with "Rhampsenit" [Rhampsenitus], a theme he found in

Herodotus. It is the tale of the thief who, having mysteriously and repeatedly broken into the royal treasure house, was made king. The outcome: "Er regierte wie die andern, / schützte Handel und Talente; / wenig, heisst es, ward gestohlen / unter seinem Regimente" ("He ruled as others do, encouraged trade and the arts; there was, it is said, very little thieving during his reign"). The poem is ironic as well as funny. And it is no coincidence that it—and with it the whole book—begins with a rollicking, infectious laugh which lasts for two stanzas and reverberates throughout the poem:

> Als der König Rhampsenit
> Eintrat in die goldne Halle
> Seiner Tochter, lachte diese,
> Lachten ihre Zofen alle.

> Auch die Schwarzen, die Eunuchen,
> Stimmten lachend ein, es lachten
> Selbst die Mumien, selbst die Sphinxe,
> Dass sie schier zu bersten dachten. (2:7)

> (When King Rhampsenitus
> Entered his daughter's golden hall,
> She was laughing,
> And all her maids were laughing too.

> The black men, the eunuchs,
> Joined in the laughter,
> Even the mummies were laughing so much, even the sphinxes,
> That they thought they would burst.)

Note the effect of the enjambment in both these stanzas. In the first, it leads to a pause, after which the full stress lands on "lachte," the key word of the whole passage. In the second instance, the equivalent emphasis on "Mumien"—"even the mummies were laughing!"— underscores the enormity of the irony. And the cause of the mirth: Not only had the thief managed to break in again but the princess who had been placed on guard—a curious idea, to be sure—had herself been "robbed":

"Ich bin keine starke Pforte
Und ich hab nicht widerstanden,
Schätzehütend diese Nacht
Kam ein Schätzlein mir abhanden."

("I am no strong gate,
And I have not withstood;
While guarding the treasure last night
A little treasure of mine got lost.")

Laughter spills over into the next poem as well. "Der weisse Elefant"
[The White Elephant, 2:10] also allows an escape into glittering,
Oriental fairyland, dealing with the unhappy love of an elephant for a
Parisian beauty. Even without recognizing, as Heine's contemporaries
would have done, in the object of his ridicule a well-known Parisian
figure, the poem is outrageously comical. Hereafter, while the irony is
undiminished, the laughter becomes less happy as tale after tale exposes
a world that is out of kilter, where cruelty and horror lurk just beneath
the gay surface. In "Schelm von Bergen" [The Scoundrel of Bergen,
2:16] the executioner—lowest of the low—is knighted; "Pfalzgräfin
Jutta" [Countess Jutta, 2:43] kills her seven lovers to ensure that they
keep their oath of fidelity. It is a world in which the base man wins, as
expressly stated in "Walküren" [Valkyries, 2:18] (This poem captures
the ride of the Valkyries so magnificently that one wonders if this is not
another motif which suggested itself to Richard Wagner through
Heine's treatment.) "Maria Antoinette" begins with a view of the gay
facade of the Tuileries whose windows sparkle in the sunlight. But
within, the specters of the past carry on a ghostly ceremonial. Maria
Antoinette is holding court, her entourage in their extravagant finery
curtsying and fawning around her, ignoring—or unaware—that they
have no heads. Buried in the burlesque charade lies a social comment.
Heine always maintained that the very society that had been guil-
lotined was still surviving—albeit without using their heads.

Despite some well-aimed barbs at identifiable targets, the satire of
Romanzero is not directed at a specific society but at the world in
general. The flaw is not in the particular event but in the world order.
Existence does not offer any hope of a happy ending: "Ich wusste, nie

komm ich gesund nach Haus" ("I knew I shall never safely return
home," 2:124). Life is a dance at the brink of a yawning abyss ("Pomare") where beauty can be saved from being sullied only by death
("Nächtliche Fahrt" [Night Journey]), where love is impossible, as in
"Der Asra":

Täglich ging die wunderschöne
Sultanstochter auf und nieder
Um die Abendzeit am Springbrunn,
Wo die weissen Wasser plätschern.

Täglich stand der junge Sklave
Um die Abendzeit am Springbrunn,
Wo die weissen Wasser plätschern;
Täglich ward er bleich und bleicher.

Eines Abends trat die Fürstin
Auf ihn zu mit raschen Worten:
"Deinen Namen will ich wissen,
Deine Heimat, deine Sippschaft!"

Und der Sklave sprach: "Ich heisse
Mohamet, ich bin aus Yemmen,
Und mein Stamm sind jene Asra,
Welche sterben, wenn sie lieben." (2:40–41)

(Every day at evening the Sultan's beautiful daughter walked up and down by
the fountain in which the white waters murmur. Every day at evening the
young slave stood by the fountain where the white waters murmur; every day
he grew more and more pale. One evening the princess came up to him with
rapid words: I wish to know your name, your home, your kin! And the slave
said: I am called Mohamet, I come from the Yemen, and my tribe are the
Asras who die when they love.)

  This is a poignant treatment not merely of one individual's unhappy
love, of which Heine had often sung before, but of the fusion of love and
death in a more profound sense.[21]
  Disappointment and deceit are the themes of "Vitziputzli" and "Der
Dichter Firdusi" [The Poet Firdusi]. Both are long, at times rambling,
but contain impressively colorful passages. Their intensity derives from

the contrast between expectation and reality, skillfully exploited by the author. "Vitziputzli" confronts the unspoiled innocence and trusting hospitality of the "barbarians" with the perfidy, greed, and cruelty of the "civilized" Spaniards. It is a story of unspeakable treachery. When Montezuma, who had hospitably welcomed the Spaniards, in turn accepts the invitation of Don Fernando Cortez, the visit ends in a bloody slaughter of the Aztecs. The Mexicans retaliate. Heine depicts it all in lurid detail, climaxing the account—very effectively—with sober statistics. Montezuma vows revenge. Not, however, in the manner in which latter-day tourists understand or experience it. Allowing his fancy to take over, the author reveals Montezuma's plan: he will continue his "career" in Europe, where he will join other pagan "gods in exile" and like them, haunt the people through their fears and prejudices.

"Der Dichter Firdusi" is the tale of the Persian poet who spends seventeen years writing his two hundred thousand verses to the glory of his country, but whom the shah cheats out of his promised reward. (Is it a coincidence that seventeen years also elapsed between the publication of *Buch der Lieder* and *Neue Gedichte?*) When the shah tries to make good his error by sending all conceivable earthly treasures, the fabulous gifts arrive just as the poet is being carried to his grave. The poem is a revealing manifestation of Heine's feelings about Uncle Salomon's betrayal. But once again, the reader need not be aware of the personal reference to appreciate the melodramatic appeal of the poem.

After this recital of pessimistic themes, I must emphasize that the poems make anything but dreary reading. On the contrary, one is struck by their vividness and ironic humor. The vitality of the creative process seems to surmount the sense of defeat. The variety of ways in which Heine externalizes his feeling about the absurdity of the universe and the malevolence of destiny—the impossibility of safe arrival—calls to mind Kafka's parabolic treatment of a similar theme. As with Kafka, personal destiny is sublimated into a vision of human existence that bears witness to a tragic view of life.

The conflict between spiritualism and sensualism, which the author has discussed previously in his prose, is now poetically embodied in "Der Apollogott" [The God Apollo], considered by some to be the centerpiece of *Historien*. The poem begins with the romantic image of the convent—not "a" convent but "the" convent—standing in solid and secure seclusion high on a rock, beneath which we literally hear the Rhine surging past:

> Das Kloster ist hoch auf Felsen gebaut,
> Der Rhein vorüberrauschet;
> Wohl durch das Gitterfenster schaut
> Die junge Nonne und lauschet. (2:30)

> (The convent is built on rocks, up high,
> The Rhine surges past;
> There, through the barred window,
> The young nun watches and listens.)

What draws the nun's attention is a boat, festooned with ribbons and flowers and a-glow in the sunset, carrying a handsome youth. Nine beautiful women, voluptuously draped in tunics, surround him while he plays the lyre and sings seductively. It is of course Apollo with his complement of muses, as perceived by the ascetic Nazarene: a sensuous tableau, a little wanton (as suggested by *Fant* ["dandy"] and *schlanke Leiber* ["slender bodies"]), but unspeakably alluring. Nor does Heine merely tell us, he shows us, through her gesture, the nun's struggling conscience:

> Ins Herz der armen Nonne dringt
> Das Lied und brennt wie Feuer.

> Sie schlägt ein Kreuz, und noch einmal
> Schlägt sie ein Kreuz, die Nonne;
> Nicht scheucht das Kreuz die süsse Qual,
> Nicht bannt es die bittre Wonne. (2:31)

> (The song pierces the heart of the poor nun
> And burns like fire.

> She crosses herself, and again
> She crosses herself, the nun;
> But the cross does not drive away the sweet pain,
> Nor exorcise the bitter delight.)

Not once but twice she crosses herself—the telling gesture and the double oxymora tell the rest.

There is a marked change in tone and mode as now we hear the song from Apollo's own lips, beginning with:

> "Ich bin der Gott der Musika,
> Verehrt in allen Landen;
> Mein Tempel hat in Grächia
> Auf Mont-Parnass gestanden". (2:31)

("I am the God of Musica,
Revered in all lands;
My temple used to stand in Greece
On Mount Parnassus".)

Having thus introduced himself, he describes the golden age in which and of which he had been singing. The lilting sounds, the obvious rhymes (falling on "Grächia" again and again) and regular cadences convey as much of the story as do the images of fairyland existence which he projects. Mixing Greek words with Latin, French and German elements, the chant has a trivializing, almost vulgarizing effect. There is a touch of self-parody as Apollo-Heine casts himself in the role of a street minstrel, a romantic crooner who suffuses everything in sweetness and glamor. As it turns out, it is the song he used to sing—a thousand years ago:

> "Wohl tausend Jahr' aus Grächia
> Bin ich verbannt, vertrieben—
> Doch ist mein Herz in Grächia,
> In Grächia geblieben". (2:32)

("Nearly a thousand years
I have been banned, expelled from Greece—
But my heart has remained in Greece,
In Greece".)

As the persona of Heine unmistakably blends with Apollo, we realize that the thrice repeated "Grächia" for which he yearns with agonizing homesickness is not so much the golden age of Hellas as the era of his youth, of health and happiness when such a sweet, glib mode of song was possible.

The third section offers yet another view of the so-called Apollo, and with it another perspective on sensuality. Here the reader is struck first of all by the change in prosody:

> In der Tracht der Beguinen,
> In dem Mantel mit der Kappe
> Von der gröbsten schwarzen Serge,
> Ist vermummt die junge Nonne. (2:32)

> (In the costume of the Bedouins
> In the hooded coat
> of roughest black serge
> The young nun is wrapped.)

The rhyme is dropped. The balladic stanza gives way to the heavier tread of the trochaic measure. Descending from her sanctuary, the young nun hurries in search of her idol. When at last she meets someone who has seen him, it is a pedlar who describes, not Phoebus Apollo, but one named Faibish, a cantor in an Amsterdam synagogue who has lost his job for his wanton behavior and who now travels about surrounded by prostitutes. One of them is called *die grüne Sau* ("the green sow"): on this jarring note ends the lecher's profile that has taken up thirteen stanzas, and the poem.

While the verbal joke—Phoebus/Faibish—may have provided the initial spark, the poem is anything but a joke. It may be read on several levels. Along with the Nazarene—Hellene dichotomy it suggests three perspectives on sensualism and also shows three faces of the poet. The reader is led to ponder on the discrepancy between reality and appearance, on the relativity of truth, and on the function of art. One may be reminded of Kafka's treatment of a similar theme, in his little vignette "Auf der Galerie" [Up in the Gallery], where the circus artist is shown from different perspectives, leaving the reader wondering which is her "true" reality: the glamorous appearance before the footlights or the sordid facts behind the scene? Or the one that makes the young spectator bury his face and cry?[22]

Heine's expertise in manipulating prosodic patterns—not for their own sake but to project and support meaning—may be similarly observed elsewhere in his late work. It becomes most obvious in those poems that are made up of several parts, as for instance in "Der Dichter

Firdusi" and "Pomare." In the former, rhymeless trochaic stanzas are
followed by an interlude of a pronounced rhyming pattern (*a b b a*),
with masculine rhymes enclosing two lines with feminine endings;
while rhymed couplets introduce a sense of urgency in the third section.
Similarly, a prosodic shift signals and conveys the changing scene of the
tetralogy "Pomare," underscoring the playgirl's rise from the gutter to
glamor and fame, and her miserable end on the dissecting table. Along
with the metric changes, literary echoes further intensify the mood.
There are (at least) two instances of this in "Pomare." Her phenomenal
rise is introduced with:

> Gestern noch fürs liebe Brot
> Wälzte sie sich tief im Kot,
> Aber heute schon mit vieren
> Fährt das stolze Weib spazieren. (2:28)

> (Yesterday she still wallowed deeply
> In the mud to earn her bread,
> To-day the proud woman
> Promenades with four horses.)

Most Germans will recall Wilhelm Hauff's well-worn song about the
fickleness of fate that begins with: "Gestern noch auf stolzen Rossen /
Heute durch die Brust geschossen" ("Yesterday still astride on proud
horses, / today shot through the chest"). The link is obviously established through the meter, just as the one in the next section which
contrasts Pomare's end with that of Goethe's "Bajadere," is based on
similarity of rhythm, tone, and wording. Whereas Goethe's prostitute
is "saved" in the last moment by her divine lover and carried "upward,"
Heine's heroine is mercifully saved by God in another way: "Bist
gerettet jetzt durch Gottes / Ew'ge Güte, du bist tot" ("You are saved
by God's eternal goodness, / you are dead"). The echo contrasts Heine's
grim realism with Goethe's happy ending.[23]

The most conspicuous formal trait of "Nächtliche Fahrt" is the
insistence on one single rhyme ("ei"), linking the first and fourth lines
throughout twelve stanzas, evidently making sure that the reader notes
that while *drei* figures embarked on their nocturnal boat ride, only *zwei*
survived. "Das goldne Kalb," which vividly brings to life the biblical
dance around the golden calf—implicit is the indictment of commer-

cialism and greed of more recent vintage—underscores the event through an intriguing prosodic variation. The usual quatrain is extended by two lines, inserted as lines four and five, their masculine endings singling them out from the rest; the shorter fifth line further stresses the shocking nature of the happening. The middle stanza goes like this:

> Hochgeschürzt bis zu den Lenden
> Und sich fassend an den Händen,
> Jungfraun edelster Geschlechter
> Kreisen wie ein Wirbelwind
> Um das Rind—
> Paukenschläge und Gelächter! (2:38)

> (Virgins from the noblest houses,
> Their skirts pulled up to their thighs,
> And holding hands,
> Circle like a whirlwind
> Around the beef—
> Drumbeats and laughter!)

A similar format serves to intensify the horror that pervades "Pfalzgräfin Jutta." But here Heine's virtuosity seems to have overshot the mark. The effect of this macabre melodrama verges on (involuntary) self-parody and brings to mind the blood-curdling burlesques of Joachim Ringelnatz or Tom Lehrer.

One of the more subtly wrought "Historien" is "Karl I" [Charles I]. While its charm may be felt even by the casual reader, a closer look will reveal some intriguing (and strangely modern) facets. The king, alone and melancholy, sits by the cradle in the charcoal-burner's hut, singing a lullaby. But before we have time to question why a king should be baby-sitting, we are caught up in the lilting, rocking strains of the song itself:

> Eiapopeia, was raschelt im Stroh?
> Es blöken im Stalle die Schafe—
> Du trägst das Zeichen an der Stirn
> Und lächelst so furchtbar im Schlafe.

> (Eiapopeia, what's rustling in the straw?
> In the stable the sheep are bleating.

On your forehead you bear the sign,
And you smile a threatening smile in your sleep.)

Or is it really a cradle-song? The poem begins with a line from a familiar nursery rhyme. The continuation also at first sounds predictable enough; "Schaf(e)," linked to "Schlaf(e)," belong, after all, to the stock phrases of the lullaby.[24] This, however, is not an infant peacefully asleep while the heavenly father tends the sheep: the sheep are bleating—the hitherto "silent majority" is evidently becoming restless; nor is this baby sweetly content: it bears "the" sign—one assumes, the mark of Kain, denoting fratricide. And as for the heavenly shepherd:

> Der alte Köhlerglaube verschwand,
> Es glauben die Köhlerkinder—
> Eiapopeia—nicht mehr an Gott,
> Und an den König noch minder.

> Das Kätzchen ist tot, die Mäuschen sind froh—
> Wir müssen zuschanden werden—
> Eiapopeia—im Himmel der Gott
> Und ich, der König auf Erden. (2:24).

> (The ancient charcoal-burner's faith is gone,
> Charcoal-burner's children no longer—
> Eiapopeia—believe in God,
> And even less in the king.

> The kitten is dead, the mice rejoice—
> We must perish—
> Eiapopeia—God in heaven
> And I, the king on earth.)

"Der alte Köhlerglaube verschwand": in the allusion to the charcoal-burner's faith, connoting childlike, unquestioning piety,[25] we once again recognize an idiom as the source of Heine's *Einfall* ("flash of thought"), and we notice and appreciate the symbolism of the setting and of the protagonists. The "Eiapopeia," as a tranquillizer for the people familiar from *Wintermärchen*,[26] also suddenly becomes meaningful as it alternately stalls and complements the king's reflections.

"Das Kätzchen ist tot" is actually a distortion of a nursery rhyme where the kitten is not dead but merely away. The king's "lullaby" transmutes the phrase into yet another formulation of the God-is-dead theme. This becomes quite clear in the next line when the world view of Charles I, who takes his divinely ordained kingship for granted, is expressed with lapidary economy. The poem's hero is of course the Charles Stuart who lost crown and head in 1649 when he clashed with the parliamentarian forces of Oliver Cromwell. It is characteristic of Heine's terse mode of writing to expect the reader to know this; Charles I becomes a symbol for the dying feudal autocracy. This cradle song, ending with "Schlaf, mein Henkerchen, schlaf" ("Sleep, my little henchman, sleep"), is, as the king knows, also his own death song. The old order goes under as the new one arises, and the tone reflects resignation and nostalgic regret. Traditional fragments and those that merely sound traditional but express the king's thoughts and fears have contrapuntally combined to give this diabolic "lullaby" its peculiar radiance and poignant appeal.

Heine's masterful manipulation of his material, which turns images, phrases, historic elements, literary echoes, and personal experience into ciphers, to be quoted and interwoven at will, has not always or everywhere been favorably received. That a poem should be artfully constructed, deliberately "made" ("ein Gedicht wird gemacht," in the words of Gottfried Benn), is a very old concept and also a fairly modern one. But nineteenth-century German scholars took a different view. The prime criterion of a poem was the degree of its genuineness as *unmittelbares Erlebnis* ("direct personal experience"), as an authentic, direct, inspired outpouring of personal feeling. By these standards, Heine's calculating craft and his awareness of the forensic impact of his work was not considered to be an asset.

Within the triadic structure of *Romanzero*, the first part is balanced by the narrative poems of the last, entitled "Hebräische Melodien" [Hebrew Melodies]—a title borrowed from Byron. The poet turns to the Jewish theme, mingling personal memories with Judaic history. There are actually only three poems in this group. "Prinzessin Sabbat" [Princess Sabbath] depicts the transformation of the work-a-day Jew from an underdog—or, as Heine suggests, someone whom the world treats like a dog—to a prince for the duration of the Sabbath. Next comes the extraordinary poem "Jehuda Ben Halevy," a paean to the Sephardic poet-philosopher of the twelfth century. With its 225 stanzas, it is Heine's longest poem (aside from the two mock epics). He calls him a troubadour whose beloved is Jerusalem, and one senses Heine's identification with his longing for a spiritual home. As is Heine's wont, he uses his subject as a frame within which to interweave a wide range of topics, slipping from the past to the present, from the pathetic to the comic, from Judaic destiny to tidbits of local gossip and returning, again and again, to the figure of his hero whose persona coalesces with his own. Despite rambling excursions and obscure allusions, it is a powerful poem containing many striking passages. Some of them are transparent in their autobiographical relevance:

> Wie im Leben, so im Dichten
> Ist das höchste Gut die Gnade—
> Wer sie hat, der kann nicht sünd'gen,
> Nicht in Versen, noch in Prosa.

> Solchen Dichter von der Gnade
> Gottes nennen wir Genie:
> Unverantwortlicher König
> Des Gedankenreiches ist er.

> Nur dem Gotte steht er Rede,
> Nicht dem Volke—In der Kunst
> Wie im Leben, kann das Volk
> Töten uns, doch niemals richten. (2:136–37)

> (In life as well as in art,
> The greatest good is [the state of] grace—
> Whoever has it, cannot sin,
> Not in verse nor in prose.

> Such a poet by the grace
> Of God we call a genius:
> He is king in the realm of thought,
> Answerable to no one.

> Only to God does he answer,
> Not to the people. In art
> As in life, the people can only
> Kill us, never judge us.)

The self-serving nature of this idealization of the "autonomous" artist would be obvious even if the author had not slipped in that first-person plural ("uns") in the last line.

Lest one think that Heine's return to God and revived interest in Judaic lore means a change of mind with regard to his contempt for what he calls positive religion, the eulogy to Jehuda Ben Halevy is followed by "Disputation," a debate between a monk and a rabbi. This spoof of the hair-splitting sophistry of theologians is a sort of satyr play, a vulgar burlesque that shows both contestants to be losers. It concludes the volume.

The middle part of *Romanzero* is taken up by the thirty-six poems of "Lamentationen" [Lamentations], including a group under the heading "Lazarus." The titles are strongly suggestive, alluding to the lament of the prophet Jeremiah and to the figure of Lazarus from the gospel of St. Luke (16:19–21), the beggar "full of sores," at the gate of the rich man.

Here—notably in the twenty pieces of the "Lazarus" cycle, in what has been called the still center—the poet takes off his masks and exposes his torment with painful directness. These poems by turn show his tenderness and his longing, his frustration and his rage, his protest and his resignation. Separated from the outside world, his imagination stimulated by reading and opiate dreams, he nevertheless remains alert and watchful, refusing to be dulled by opium for any length of time. He manages to reveal in realistic detail aspects of the human experience as they have never before been expressed in literature—either because poets avoided them or because there never has been a case like his where, as he put it, poetry has remained his most faithful friend, following him to the edge of the grave and fighting with death for him.

It is remarkable how many changes Heine can ring on the theme of existential anguish and, at the same time, on the possibilities of comic release. In his early poetry, ironic turnabouts had not only served to show the romanticism of others to be hollow but also to hold his own sentimentality at bay; now his wit saves his poetry from becoming depressing or maudlin. His ability to show the other side passes the supreme test: even the terrible reality of his disintegration and approaching death is neither evaded nor diminished, yet still suffused with humor. It is the frankness of his complaint together with his ability to laugh about it which gives his late poems their singular quality.

Take, for instance, his gentle refusal to accept platitudinous comfort in "Rückschau" [Retrospect]. Having drawn a heartrending comparison between the blissful past and the present nightmare, he makes the grave almost seem a welcome place of respite after all the hassle, and death almost a redeemer—but only almost: the hint of irony at the very last does not admit such easy way out.

> Jetzt bin ich müd' vom Rennen und Laufen,
> Jetzt will ich mich im Grabe verschnaufen.
> Lebt wohl! Dort oben, ihr christlichen Brüder,
> Ja, das versteht sich, dort sehn wir uns wieder. (2:109)

> (Now I am tired from all that rushing and running,
> Now I want to catch my breath in the grave.
> Farewell! Up there, you Christian brothers,
> We shall, yes of course, see each other again.)

The parenthetical aside—"ja, das versteht sich"—makes a world of difference, disposing of the Christian promise as a pious cliché.

Among the several poems which convey the poet's affectionate concern for Mathilde, one of the best known and most touching is "Gedächtnisfeier" [Memorial day]:

> Keine Messe wird man singen,
> Keinen Kadosch wird man sagen,
> Nichts gesagt und nichts gesungen
> Wird an meinen Sterbetagen.
>
> Doch vielleicht an solchem Tage,
> Wenn das Wetter schön und milde,
> Geht spazieren auf Montmartre
> Mit Paulinen Frau Mathilde.
>
> Mit dem Kranz von Immortellen
> Kommt sie, mir das Grab zu schmücken,
> Und sie seufzet: "Pauvre homme!"
> Feuchte Wehmut in den Blicken.
>
> Leider wohn ich viel zu hoch,
> Und ich habe meiner Süssen

Keinen Stuhl hier anzubieten;
Ach! sie schwankt mit müden Füssen.

Süsses, dickes Kind, du darfst
Nicht zu Fuss nach Hause gehen;
An dem Barrieregitter
Siehst du die Fiaker stehen. (2:116)

(No mass will be sung,
No kaddish said,
Nothing will be said or sung
On the anniversaries of my death.

But perhaps on such a day,
When the weather is fine and mild,
Frau Mathilde will go for a walk
On Montmartre with Pauline.

With a wreath of immortelles
She will come to adorn my grave,
And sigh: Pauvre homme!,
A moist sadness in her eye.

Unfortunately I live much too high up,
And I have no chair
To offer my sweet one;
Alas, she totters on weary feet.

Sweet, fat child,
You mustn't walk home;
You'll see the coaches
Standing at the gate.)

As so often, one must admire Heine's skill in exploiting contrasts.
The prospect of utter bleakness and oblivion (effected through the
fourfold negation and the alliteration of harsh or hissing *k*— and
s—sounds as much as by the statement which makes him an outcast
even in death), is suddenly replaced by the anticipated presence of
Mathilde's warm, plump, simple humanity; the rituals which he has
scorned seem remote and abstract compared to his wife's "immortelles." "Immortelles"—a fortuitously suggestive, mellifluent

name for the "everlasting," strawlike Xeranthenum annuum! Her "pauvre homme"—an expression Heine must have heard time after time from her lips—incidentally reminds us that for Mathilde, he was not an immortal German poet but her poor sick man. His cavalier regret of being unable to offer her a chair because his abode is so high up, his generous insistence that she return home by cab, together with the information where she may get one, captures the quality of their relationship while simultaneously injecting a gentle touch of irony: Heine pokes fun at himself for carrying his fatherly concern for his "sweet, fat child" even beyond the grave. Also: in life, he called her his *Verbrengerin* ("spendthrift"); now he can afford to be generous!

So compelling was Heine's identification with the figure of the biblical Lazarus that he returned to it again in a later group of eleven poems entitled "Zum Lazarus" (in *Gedichte 1853 und 1854*). The first of these asks the hardest question of all:

Lass die heil'gen Parabolen,
Lass die frommen Hypothesen—
Suche die verdammten Fragen
Ohne Umschweif uns zu lösen.

Warum schleppt sich blutend, elend,
Unter Kreuzlast der Gerechte,
Während glücklich als ein Sieger
Trabt auf hohem Ross der Schlechte?

Woran liegt die Schuld? Ist etwa
Unser Herr nicht ganz allmächtig?
Oder treibt er selbst den Unfug?
Ach, das wäre niederträchtig.

Also fragen wir beständig,
Bis man uns mit einer Handvoll
Erde endlich stopft die Mäuler—
Aber ist das eine Antwort? (2:209)

(Never mind the holy parables,
Never mind the pious hypotheses—
Try to solve these damned questions
Without beating around the bush.

Why does the just man drag himself, bleeding and wretched,
Beneath the weight of the cross,
While the scoundrel trots
On his high horse, the happy victor?

Where does the fault lie? Is perhaps
Our Lord not quite omnipotent?
Or is he himself the troublemaker?
Ah, that would be vile.

So we constantly ask,
Till finally they shut our traps
With a handful of earth—
But is that an answer?)

The reconciliation of evil and pain with divine justice, benevolence,
and omnipotence has occupied theologians ever since Jeremiah asked
his "Wherefore doth the way of the wicked prosper?" But when has the
question been formulated so urgently and simply, and flung out with
such defiant reproach? The poem hardly requires any elucidation. But it
invites the reader, once again, to observe Heine's knack for enhancing
meaning by the manipulation of meter, image, and rhyme. Dismissing
all traditional attempts at glossing over the crucial question by pious or
learned palliation, he lets the first accent twice crash on the imperative
"lass" and then with equal contempt, on the questioning or deprecating
conjunctions ("warum," "woran," "während," "oder," to the final
"aber"). The contrast between the two visions confronted in the second
stanza is made still more crass by the rhyme which links "Gerechte" and
"Schlechte," just as in the following quatrain "allmächtig" is made to
rhyme with "niederträchtig" in a near blasphemous agreement. Thus
attuned to expect the rhyme, we are let down at the end: "Aber ist das
eine Antwort?" ("Handvoll—Antwort," despite the agreement of the
vowels, hardly provides a satisfying rhyme.) The piece concludes with a
jarring, unrhymed question—to suggest that life is without rhyme or
reason is precisely Heine's point.

     At times the poet assumes an air of humility that is deeply moving,
despite the humorous tinge. He says he is willing to forego the much
praised heavenly pastures—he does not particularly fancy sitting on
clouds and singing psalms anyway—in exchange for a little more of this

so-called vale of tears; all he asks of the Lord is better health and a raise
in salary ("Geldzulage"):

> Genieren wird das Weltgetreibe
> Mich nie, denn selten geh ich aus;
> In Schlafrock und Pantoffeln bleibe
> Ich gern bei meiner Frau zu Haus. (2:216)

> (The world's bustle will not bother me,
> For I seldom go out;
> In my housecoat and slippers,
> I like to stay at home with my wife.)

The Philistine pleasures which as a young man he ridiculed, now seem
ultimate bliss.

Looking back, he recalls triumphs and pleasures, but also old hurts
and grievances, as for instance in "Affrontenburg" [Castle of Affronts,
2:206], which harks back to insults suffered in Hamburg. Yet despite
the preoccupation with himself, brought about by sickness and isolation and aggravated still further by the near-blindness which interfered
with his reading as well, numerous poems attest to his continuing
interest in world affairs. Social comment is contained in a group of
charming verse fables and in miscellaneous satirical pieces. "Das
Sklavenschiff" [The Slave Ship, 2:201] describes in grim detail the
calculating greed and cruelty of the slave traders and the plight of their
victims. In mid-journey, the captain notes the mounting death toll
among his human cargo. Alarmed because he fears a cut in his profit, he
plans a remedy: the prisoners are to be allowed on deck for a dance.
There ensues an extraordinary spectacle, described with Heine's characteristic attention to lurid detail. With frenzied abandon, the doomed
men perform a Bacchanalian dance, at the very edge of the deep, while
hungry sharks are waiting below. Suddenly, the reader realizes that the
ordeal of the slaves also stands for human suffering in general and that
the rapacious selfishness of "Superkargo Mynheer van Koek" represents
insatiable commercialism and corruption; the dance of the slaves has
turned into a disturbing symbol of human existence.

Perhaps the most celebrated of Heine's political poems was considered too potent to be included in the volumes published in his lifetime:
"Die schlesischen Weber" [The Silesian Weavers] was written in 1844,

immediately after the weavers' rebellion in the Silesian towns of Peterswaldau and Langenbielau had been squashed by troops. The piece appeared in *Vorwärts!* in July, 1844, and soon found its way into Germany in clandestine circulation.[27] Friedrich Engels translated it into English. The weavers' plight became the topic of poems by several authors[28] and, a generation later, still had incendiary impact when Gerhart Hauptmann dramatized it and Käthe Kollwitz depicted it in her famous drawings.

> Im düstern Auge keine Träne,
> Sie sitzen am Webstuhl und fletschen die Zähne:
> "Deutschland, wir weben dein Leichentuch,
> Wir weben hinein den dreifachen Fluch—
>   Wir weben, wir weben!

> Ein Fluch dem Gotte, zu dem wir gebeten
> In Winterskälte und Hungersnöten;
> Wir haben vergebens gehofft und geharrt,
> Er hat uns geäfft und gefoppt und genarrt—
>   Wir weben, wir weben!

> Ein Fluch dem König, dem König der Reichen,
> Den unser Elend nicht konnte erweichen,
> Der den letzten Groschen von uns erpresst,
> Und uns wie Hunde erschiessen lässt—
>   Wir weben, wir weben!

> Ein Fluch dem falschen Vaterlande,
> Wo nur gedeihen Schmach und Schande,
> Wo jede Blume früh geknickt,
> Wo Fäulnis und Moder den Wurm erquickt—
>   Wir weben, wir weben!

> Das Schiffchen fliegt, der Webstuhl kracht,
> Wir weben emsig Tag und Nacht—
> Altdeutschland, wir weben dein Leichentuch,
> Wir weben hinein den dreifachen Fluch,
>   Wir weben, wir weben!" (2:343–44)

(No tears in their somber eyes,
They sit at the loom and bare their teeth:
"Germany, we are weaving your shroud,

We are weaving into it the triple curse—
We are weaving, we are weaving!

A curse on the God to whom we prayed
In the cold of winter and in time of famine;
We have hoped and waited in vain,
He has mocked and fooled and deluded us—
We are weaving, we are weaving!

A curse on the king, the king of the rich,
Whom our wretchedness could not move,
Who extorts our last penny from us,
And has us shot down like dogs—
We are weaving, we are weaving!

A curse on our false fatherland,
Where only disgrace and shame flourish,
Where every flower is soon broken,
Where rot and decay nourish the worm—
We are weaving, we are weaving!

The shuttle flies, the loom creaks,
We are weaving busily day and night—
Old Germany, we are weaving your shroud,
Into it we weave the triple curse,
We are weaving, we are weaving!")

An important asset of this poem is its terseness. The poet does not waste words on explanations, but takes familiarity with the circumstances for granted and simply assumes the voice of the victims. The piece is held together by a telling image: the weavers, dry-eyed—tears after all have a relieving, softening effect—are sitting at their looms, weaving their thoughts of mutinous desperation as they work on "Old-Germany's shroud." The triple curse alludes to the Prussian military slogan that exhorts the faithful to serve God, king, and fatherland. One by one, all three are exposed as hollow, treacherous idols. The meter suggests the weaving motion, imbuing it with an archetypal, almost mythical, aura: the refrain sounds more ominous with every reprise, and the weavers' sense of disillusion and rebellion becomes ever more urgent.

When it was first published, entitled "Die armen Weber" [The Poor Weavers], the piece ended with the fourth stanza. It is easy to see why the poet added a fifth stanza, which counterbalances the opening and thus completes the frame, so to speak, with the repeat of the curse—all of which undeniably intensifies the effect. But Heine made another change, the reason for which is not quite so obvious, involving the first two lines of the second stanza. Originally they read: "Ein Fluch dem Gotte, dem blinden, tauben, / Zu dem wir gebetet mit kindlichem Glauben" ("A curse on the blind and deaf God / to whom we have prayed in childlike faith," 2:637). The next two lines, with their onomatopoetic parody, remained unchanged. What induced the poet to alter the two lines, even though the "improved" version has a less clean rhyme ("gebeten," "nöten") and introduces the grammatically incorrect "gebeten"? This form is the past of *bitten* ("to beg"), but it does not go with "zu." Did the poet perhaps mean the speech of the uneducated, naive believer to suggest a blend of the two meanings which restores to the ritual of *beten* ("pray") some of the urgency of *bitten* with which it is etymologically allied? This curious, seemingly deliberate blemish aside, the original version describes God as deaf and blind and the people's faith as childlike. It states explicitly what the final version merely implies yet at the same time forcefully demonstrates, with heightened effect. This, by the way, is one poem without any hint of ironic deflation.

It goes without saying that Heine's poetic fables are filled with irony and satire, and are far from offering the single-minded moral ("Moral von der Geschicht") commonly associated with the genre. "Die Wanderratten" [Migratory Rats] has a message at once powerful and ambivalent.[29] Written after 1848 when the Paris Revolution had sent shivers of panic through Europe, this "fable" converts Heine's warnings about communism—uttered previously in reports to the *Augsburg Allgemeine Zeitung*—into an image of a horde of hungry rats advancing upon a town while the burgomaster and senate prepare to stem the tide with speeches, prayers, and guns. The poem begins with:

Es gibt zwei Sorten Ratten:
Die hungrigen und die satten.
Die satten bleiben vergnügt zu Haus,
Die hungrigen aber wandern aus. (2:392)

(There are two kinds of rats:
The hungry and the fat.
The fat ones stay happily at home
But the hungry ones set out to roam.)

The strong march-beat captures the inevitability as well as the mounting menace of the rats' advance. Their threat is brilliantly conveyed in two pregnant puns:

Es haben diese Käuze
Gar fürchterliche Schnäuze;
Sie tragen die Köpfe geschoren egal,
Ganz radikal, ganz rattenkahl. (2:392)

(These queer fellows
Have terrifying snouts
[or: Are terrible big-mouths, in a figurative sense];
They wear their heads shorn equally,
Quite radical, quite rat-bald.
[The pun "rattenkahl-ratzekahl" defies translation.]

Although the portrayal of the rats is anything but flattering, Heine's tongue-in-cheek description of the defenders distances him from them as well. The insistent march-beat meanwhile has given way to a measure more appropriately reflecting their frantic and futile activity:

Heute helfen euch nicht die Wortgespinste
Der abgelebten Redekünste.
Man fängt nicht Ratten mit Syllogismen,
Sie springen über die feinsten Sophismen.
Im hungrigen Magen Eingang finden
Nur Suppenlogik mit Knödelgründen.

(The verbal tricks of worn rhetoric
Will not help you today.
You can't catch rats with syllogisms,
They jump over the finest sophisms.
Only soup-logic with reason-dumplings
Gain access to a hungry stomach.)

This ambivalence is not so much a sign of instability or insecurity as of sophistication. While the optimistic sons of the Enlightenment—

young Heine among them—tended to believe that justice, freedom, and beauty go hand in hand and would eventually be achieved by rational endeavor, the disillusioned, wiser Heine knew—as do his twentieth-century readers—that the best we may hope for is a precarious balance which requires choices and sacrifice. To further social justice, some measure of freedom must be surrendered, and vice versa. Just how fully and clearly he appreciated this dilemma, Heine demonstrates in the famous passage, already cited, with which he introduced the French edition of Lutetia (2:247).

Fairy-Tale Ending? "La Mouche"

One of the "Lazarus" poems, with somewhat of an understatement, concludes: "Unjung und nicht mehr ganz gesund, / wie ich es bin zu dieser Stund', / möcht' ich noch einmal lieben, schwärmen / und glücklich sein—doch ohne Lärmen" (Un-young and no longer completely healthy as I am at this time, I should once more like to be in love, infatuated, happy—but without much noise, 2:114). This wish was to be granted—perhaps mainly because the poet strongly wished it—when in the summer 1855 a young woman called on him with some sheets of music. A warm friendship developed which was to brighten the last eight months of Heine's life.

The woman's legal name was Elise Krinitz but she used various other names: Margot, Margareth, and later, as a nom de plume, Camille Selden.[30] She seems to have deliberately surrounded herself with an aura of mystery, possibly to cover up her illegitimate origin. It is now assumed that she was born in Prague as the daughter of a governess in the house of Count Nostitz and was brought to Paris by her German foster parents. Whatever her background or name, to Heine she was his beloved "La Mouche," after the fly-shaped seal she used on her letters. (In addition, like Crescence, Elise Krinitz "scratched [his] throat." Heine found soft-sounding names—all, incidentally, beginning with M, as does Mutter—for all three important women in his life: Molly, Mathilde, Mouche.) "La Mouche" performed some secretarial duties but above all she was a sympathetic friend whom Heine showered with declarations of his affection. Evidently responsive to his feelings, she brought a singular sense of fulfillment into his final year: celebrated poet of love-lyrics that he was, and one intensely concerned with his self-image, he could see his life and career coming full circle. Just as he had visualized King Solomon, in one of the most beautiful poems of "Lazarus" (the one which, significantly, follows the above quoted lines) drawing life from the bond to his Sulamith, so he, Heine, comes emotionally alive again. He addressed twenty-five letters and six poems to "La Mouche," spicing his tender declarations with ironic regrets at being reduced to expressing his love through poems alone. Foremost among them is the one generally entitled "Für die Mouche" [For la Mouche]. It is his swan song, reportedly written two weeks before his death.

It is an extraordinary poem. Despite its length—it consists of thirty-seven stanzas of majestically flowing iambic pentameters with crossed rhymes—it is not at all rambling. With a great sweep of composition and inner coherence, it gathers in the fundamental concerns that have occupied him throughout his life, projecting them with vivid intensity and undiminished poetic power. Beginning in the midst of a dream, the scene is one of devastation, with fragmented remains of sculptures from different cultures and periods strewn about, all ravaged "by time, the worst syphilis of all." A man is seen entombed in a stone sarcophagus that is embellished by a weird mixture of mythological figures. These bas-reliefs obviously symbolize the various strains of European tradition, Judeo-Christian and Hellenic sources of Heine's inspiration, and the conflict between them; while the ivy which has overgrown and entwined them, suggests the German-romantic component. Embedded in and embraced by this allegorical presentation is a luminous love story: an unspoken dialogue between the sleeping man and the "passion flower" above his head. This flower, which according to folklore bears in its chalice the torture instruments used in Christ's passion, embodies Heine's favorite oxymoron, the bittersweet blend of love and pain. The silent colloquy between the flower and the sleeper is interrupted when a noisy quarrel erupts between the statuary, in a dispute between "truth" and "beauty":

> Oh, dieser Streit wird enden nimmermehr,
> Stets wird die Wahrheit hadern mit dem Schönen,
> Stets wird geschieden sein der Menschheit Heer
> In zwei Partei'n: Barbaren und Hellenen. (2:450)

(Alas, this dispute will never end,
Truth will forever be at odds with beauty,
Mankind will always be divided
Into two parties: Barbarians and Hellenes.)

The poem ends when the braying of the ass of Balaam drowns out the dispute. As elsewhere in Heine's late work, the ass stands for the malevolent stupidity which he sees all around him outshouting what is beautiful and worthwhile.

Heine wrote several profoundly moving terminal poems that could be chosen to express his farewell. One of his beautiful longer pieces is "Bimini." It follows Don Juan Ponce de Leon (the discoverer of Florida) in his search for the fountain of youth. When at last he finds the magic well of peace and eternal bliss, it is the river of death:

Lethe heisst das gute Wasser!
Trink daraus, und du vergisst
All dein Leiden—ja, vergessen
Wirst du, was du je gelitten—

Gutes Wasser! gutes Land!
Wer dort angelangt, verlässt es
Nimmermehr—denn dieses Land
Ist das wahre Bimini. (2:477)

(The good water is called Lethe!
Drink from it and you forget
All your suffering—yes, you will forget
All that ever pained you—

Good water! good country!
Whoever arrives there, will never
Leave it—for this country
Is the true Bimini.)

Chapter Eight
Legacy and Aftermath

To make a summary judgment about Heine's intellectual legacy in a few sentences is virtually impossible. Not only the dilemma within him but also his change of opinion when circumstances changed, caused him to take seemingly contradictory positions that are perplexing unless one keeps in mind the context in which a given statement was made.[1] It is possible, however, to point to some consistent traits of his style.

Perhaps its most striking feature is its concreteness. Heine is a master in conveying abstract thought in concrete terms and in making us aware of humdrum reality as if with new eyes. The tendency to express things through images, as evidenced in the idiom of proverbs or in the language of children or cultural primitives, is sometimes ascribed to simple minds. But Heine's use of metaphor has the opposite effect, suggesting intensive cerebral activity and a great capacity for abstraction: an agile, lively intellect at work that can reach into a prodigious stock of remembered facts and summon evidence seemingly at will. Through the metaphor, the author points out the congruence of two disparate images in their central aspects of meaning. The reader, attempting to follow his train of thought, to "get the point" of the comparison, is made aware of facts (aspects, notions, truths) that he may have been unaware of, have overlooked, or taken for granted—in short, Heine takes his reader on a journey of discovery although he seems to travel on familiar ground; a journey, moreover, that is continually punctuated by revealing flashes of wit.

With farfetched, sometimes bizarre analogies Heine may fulfill a function similar to that of latter-day political cartoonists: to present while at the same time illuminating and diagnosing, fusing presentation with analysis. Therein lies a certain danger. Metaphors may be charged with a subliminal import. Without proving anything, they act as persuaders—as modern advertisers know only too well—and as

Heine himself put it in his inimitable, metaphoric way: "Das Wort umarmt dich, während der Gedanke dich küsst" ("The word embraces you while the thought kisses you," 5:286). Nor are his metaphors always recognizable as such, since anything is grist for his metaphoric mill: not only obvious similes but all sorts of episodic elements, fictitious or factual, consisting of a phrase or a whole anecdote, are craftily interwoven into a collage or linked into an associative chain. The reader, never knowing where the author is about to lead him, is required to be alert—in a word, he feels stimulated. But the blurring of boundaries between fact and fiction, between the literal and the figurative, between objective and subjective "truth," between the serious and the comic, has made Heine suspect in the eyes of some. It is a problem with which readers in the second half of the twentieth century are not unfamiliar.

It is noteworthy, but not surprising, that despite his incessant employment of metaphors Heine rarely (perhaps never?) mixed them. "Aus dem Bilde fallen"—to fall out of the picture—is the graphic German term for the sort of lapse for which Karl Gutzkow was notorious. A writer or speaker will mix his metaphors when he has lost his sense of their literal meaning. It is not surprising that Heine was not guilty of this, precisely because he was so profoundly aware of etymological roots. It is this awareness which kept him from indiscriminately piling up tropes—instead, as we have seen earlier, he tended to expand and enhance whatever image he had chosen. The same awareness made him resuscitate many dead metaphors and return to a worn idiom its original freshness.

The concreteness (Anschaulichkeit) and vividness of Heine's speech, together with its seemingly natural flow, has had a liberating influence on German literary language, making it a more sensitive and flexible medium, better reflecting the natural tone, idiom, and gesture of the spoken word. It is all the more remarkable that Heine should have contributed to the regeneration and enrichment of his mother tongue while being cut off from the German environment for twenty-five years, that is, for the better part of his adult life.

His effectiveness partly derives also from the fact that he never loses sight of the reader: not only does he address him frequently, but more importantly, he envisions his point of view and, more often than not, manipulates it by assuming a certain perspective as a foil against which whatever point he wishes to make will stand out all the more starkly. Exploitation of contrast is, in fact, another outstanding trait of Heine's style. Antithetical thinking is basic to him: ideas, forces, events, and people divide into friendly and hostile ones. This tendency of viewing the world in terms of opposites pervades his writing technique as well. As he articulated it in the preface to *Salon,* volume 1: "Just as the quality of spring can best be recognized in winter, so love of freedom is a prison flower; only in prison does one fully appreciate the value of freedom" (4:592). Like any painter, or any good raconteur, Heine is aware of the importance of a contrasting frame for the effect of the picture, of the appropriate frame of mind for the success of a tale. There is hardly a page in his work where he does not demonstrate his knack for "framing": by creating an effective viewing angle by alluding to contrary expectations, or by simply juxtaposing contrasting phenomena. It is a form of alienation—just as metaphoric presentation is—to counteract the blinkers with which familiarity equips us, and makes us see afresh. Or rather, experience afresh, for he involves all our senses, the gustatory and olfactory as well as the aural and visual. And is the contrast between our expectation and some surprising turn not ultimately the basis of most jokes?

Finally there is the already described mimetic function of Heine's language, the slight-of-hand by which he makes the sentences do what they talk about, achieved through the interaction of syntactic structure, semantic and metaphoric content, and sound effects. It may be observed in his prose as well as in his verse. An example is the passage which shows Luther standing before the Council of Worms: "Es war ein wehmütiges Geständnis, wenn der arme Mönch, der vor Kaiser und Reich zu Worms angeklagt stand, ob seiner Lehre, dennoch, trotz aller Demut seines Herzens, jeden Widerruf für unmöglich erklärte und mit den Worten schloss: 'Hier stehe ich, ich kann nicht anders, Gott helfe mir. Amen!' " ("It was a sad confession when the poor monk, who stood at Worms before emperor and realm, accused because of his teaching, nonetheless, despite his heartfelt humility, declared any recantation to be impossible and concluded with the words: 'Here I stand, I cannot do otherwise, God help me, Amen!' " 4:586). The infinitely awkward, indeed impossible sentence (offered in a student's composition, it would be annihilated by red ink) captures Luther's agonized groping and "holy compulsion." Incidentally, "die heilige Zwingnis," as the context reveals, is also meant to allude to the situation of the poet.

One becomes especially aware of Heine's tightly controlled, dense speech patterns when attempting to translate him. Complimented by a visitor on the dazzling, captivating quality of his style, he is quoted to have replied: "But you wouldn't believe how much work and trouble [*Mühe und Arbeit*] this style gives me."[2] It is one of the ironies of Heine's reception in Germany that he was to be blamed in some quarters for the deterioration of the German language! With this, we come to the "aftermath."

Heine is said to have been the most talked about and controversial German writer of his day, perhaps the first who had the status of a public figure. And neither his fame nor his notoriety faded after his death. His rocky posthumous career, full of ironic turns and surprising anomalies, seems more eventful than his life had been.

That their "Henri Heine" should have occupied a special place in the consciousness of the French is not surprising, not only because he lived among them for twenty-five years. He had arranged for the prompt translation of his works into French, and in some instances the French version appeared before the German, and without mutilation by the censor. French historians reportedly consider him the most reliable witness of the July monarchy[3] and his profound influence on Baudelaire and the symbolists is well documented.[4] Visitors to his grave have usually found it bedecked with fresh flowers. Today, the Bibliothèque nationale is one of the major depositories of Heineana, and French scholars are coeditors, together with their German counterparts, of the critical Heine edition now underway in Düsseldorf.

More surprising is the high regard in which Heine has been held by the English, ever since he was introduced to them through Matthew Arnold's famous essay,[5] followed by George Eliot's effusive eulogy. This popularity reached a peak in the Victorian period.[6] His almost legendary fame in England is all the more remarkable in view of his dislike of the English which he repeatedly vented in caustic—though penetrating and highly amusing—comments. His English readers perceived in him an enemy of political and ecclesiastical tyranny and a critic of aristocratic privilege and Philistine narrowness. They liked his cosmopolitan, humanitarian, liberal attitude but, above all, they savored his wit. His works were widely translated and even imitated.[7] It was in the English speaking countries that the revival of interest in Heine following the end of World War II had its beginning, when the long established respect for Heine combined with the special regard which exiles from Hitler's Germany felt for the author of "Denk ich an Deutschland in der Nacht."[8] Several of the studies originating in England or North America broke new ground and helped promote the unprecedented resurgence of interest which has not yet subsided.

While Israel would not name a street after him,[9] Jews on the whole have no difficulty identifying with him. In spite of his rejection of Jewish orthodoxy along with any other religious doctrine or ritual, he is viewed as having "remained in the deepest reaches of his soul a Jew."[10] Critical of most of the Jews with whom he came in contact and especially of the Hamburg commercial circles, he always treated Judaic lore and traditions with affectionate reverence, and his Jewish allegiance and sympathies came strongly to the fore when confronted with anti-Semitism.

In other European countries—in Spain, Scandinavia, Hungary, and among Slavic nations—Heine is admired as the foremost German poet, surpassed only by Goethe. He is one of the few writers of modern times—some say the only one[11]—to have achieved international fame chiefly on the basis of lyrical poetry, a genre more than any other tied to its original medium.

In his homeland, the story of Heine's *Aufnahme* ("reception") is an altogether different one. The *Buch der Lieder,* immensely popular and widely imitated,[12] was the best-seller of the nineteenth century, second only to the Bible, whereas his prose tended to be read and appreciated by a more select public. Among those who are known to have valued him highly and in fact often quote him are such architects of modern European thought as Marx, Nietzsche, Freud, and Jung.[13]

Nietzsche in particular seems to have been strongly influenced by Heine and the catalog of shared ideas and attitudes is surprisingly long: his critique of Christianity and revaluation of Western society's traditional values; the notion (and image) of the death of God; the discovery of Dionysus as a vital, creative force, and the antithesis of cognitive and creative capacities expressed in terms of Apollonian-Dionysian polarity; the critical judgment on romanticism; the interpretation of Luther's reformation as a "peasants' revolt of the spirit"

(*Bauernaufstand des Geistes*); the perspectivist view, in contrast to faith in absolutes; the psychological notions of repression, of rationalization and sublimation, and of *ressentiment;* the occupation with dreams as masks, the recognition of the dominant role of the subconscious—in short, the beginnngs of depth psychology; the categories of *Herren-mensch* and *Herdenmensch* (the sovereign individual versus mob rule), and the anticipation of a stronger and emotionally better balanced (and therefore healthier) "new" kind of man; the appreciation of dance as a primal expression of emotions; the preference for a peculiar blend of laughter and tears; last but not least, the cosmopolitanism, coupled with a love-hate relationship with Germany. (Paradoxical as it may seem, even Nietzsche's much publicized misogyny—for which existentially he probably needed no model—can be traced back to Heine, the supreme writer of love songs!) All of these notions and attitudes, which have become known as central tenets of Nietzsche's thinking and as such have entered modern consciousness, are anticipated and prefigured in Heine's work. Heine's influence on Nietzsche—never acknowledged, although Nietzsche made no secret of his admiration for Heine—is all the more interesting if one compares the different place which Heine held in the minds of Germans during the first half of this century to that of Nietzsche; Nietzsche's ideas (as distorted by his National-Socialist admirers) were acclaimed in support of the very attitudes which would have erased all memory of Heine.[14]

The vilification had started well before the Hitler era. The centenary of Heine's birth found his admirers and his detractors embroiled in a *Denkmalstreit* ("memorial controversy"), an acrimonious quarrel as to whether or not Heine deserved to be commemorated by a statue. An allegorical fountain, commissioned by his supporters—most prominent among them Empress Elisabeth of Austria—had actually been completed. But so fierce was the opposition to its placement anywhere in Germany that the sculpture was sent into exile. It has since found a home in the Bronx. Undaunted, Empress Elisabeth ordered a bust of Heine which, she hoped, would seem less subversive than the allegorical Loreley fountain, but it too was not deemed acceptable in Germany and later graced the Isle of Korfu. Heine's fans responded by publishing a printed memorial instead, a collection of laudatory testimonials in prose and verse by German intellectuals and literati.[15] This uproar, worthy to be the subject of a comic opera (or of Heine's satire), was symptomatic of the abiding resentment of official Germany, an antagonism which especially surfaced in periods marked by patriotic fervor and "Teutomaniac" narrowness: in the years immediately following Heine's death, in the 1870s, at the turn of the century, and, of course, in the Hitler era when an attempt was made to snuff out the poet's memory completely.[16] The poet who had loved Germany with a moving intensity, offended German sensibility perhaps more than any other author. He was resented because he was different, Francophile, ironic, and, worst of all, a Jew. Even when his work was criticized, it was his person—his ambivalence, his frivolousness, his self-assurance, his vanity, his rootlessness—that was under attack. In the words of a prominent historian of German ideology: "the Jew was [also] viewed as embodying rootlessness, the force most antagonistic to völkisch values. . . . The increasingly violent attacks on Heinrich Heine during the late nineteenth century merit attention in this context, for Heine came to symbolize the rootlessness of the Jew. . . . 'One never knows where one is with him.'"[17]

Heine had been the "great exception"[18] in his own time, refusing to identify with any group, party, or literary movement. While it is not uncommon for outstanding personalities to be considered outsiders within their lifetime, they usually are assimilated into the mainstream of tradition sooner or later. Shocking heretics in the eyes of contemporaries often appear fairly tame, if perhaps somewhat quaint, to succeeding generations. Not so in the case of Heine, whose capacity to arouse passionate responses did not seem to diminish with passing time. What complicates the record of his colorful posthumous career even further is an opposition to him which has little to do with reactionary politics or anti-Semitism. Even judgments apparently based on literary criteria tended not merely to differ—there would be nothing extraordinary about that—but to diverge so strongly as to be polarized, either acclaiming him as one of the world's greats, a "European event" as Nietzsche put it,[19] or rejecting him as a charlatan, a *Gaukler* (buffoon or fraud), a nuisance, and a scandal.[20] Heine's most outstanding twentieth-century critic was the Austrian Karl Kraus, himself a converted Jew and anything but a chauvinist. His indictment is contained in the much-quoted essay "Heine und die Folgen" [Heine and the Consequences, 1910].[21] Kraus faulted Heine's songs for being all-too-imitable, accused him of treating serious subjects with levity, and ultimately blamed him for the ills and sins of modern journalism.[22] This negative view by the highly respected Karl Kraus—who, incidentally, shows great affinity with Heine in many ways—carried considerable weight for several decades and made Heine an easy target. The following excerpt, from a letter by Stefan Zweig to Emil Ludwig, will show how Heine's admirers felt themselves to be dissenters from the prevailing judgment. After expressing his apprehension about Germany's future—the letter was written in November, 1918—Zweig says: "and all this has been set down already, in the divinely prophetic prose of the much derided and despised [*des verlachten und verachteten*] Heinrich Heine: to read it today is pure magic. How he knew this people and the others, too, and how he loved them all, the magnificent Jewish European, who, in spite of everything [*trotz allem und allem*] is our spiritual father and model! Why did we disregard him, the journalist, why did we not read and believe him? He had more to say to us than all the wise men [*die Wissenden*] of today."[23]

Yet another circumstance tends to make Heine into a "case." He was a symbolic figure not only to his enemies; to his friends Heine's personality is also likely to be more memorable than his work.[24] His image has been transformed into a myth, partly started by himself, but accentuated by the manner in which his public reacted to him, and intensified in the course of time. Both the extravagant praise of his fans and the condemnation of his opponents have imbued Heine's name with a symbolic significance which has persisted up to the present. One of the events which commemorated the one hundred and seventy-fifth year of his birth in 1972 was the publication of a book containing responses of ninety contemporary German authors who had been asked what Heinrich Heine meant to them.[25] It makes fascinating reading. That the question should have been asked in the first place says something about Heine's unique position. In reading the colorful assortment of comments and anecdotes brimming with affection, of nostalgic recollections, defiant statements, and reflective outpourings, one becomes increasingly aware of a Heine whose memory is not only alive but exerts a very special radiance; this despite the fact that for the generation of Germans who grew up in the 1930s his name had been erased from the books. Despite—or perhaps also because of it? For what most of these otherwise so disparate responses seem to have in common is the view of Heine as a rallying symbol for free spirits and for those who cherish ideals that place them in opposition to oppressive despotism. Identification with Heine somehow signals a commitment to a free and larger community of man.

It is no coincidence, therefore, that after the collapse of the Third Reich, when German and French youth came together in a memorable encounter to pledge reconciliation and brotherhood, the locale for this gathering was the Rock of the Loreley, a place that derives its significance from its association with Heine's name. It was this meeting on the Rock of the Loreley which founded the *Europa-Haus* movement to promote the idea of a New Europe in a concrete and practical way by helping young people to overcome the confines of nationalism.

Other examples of Heine's continuing role as a touchstone for reactions take us even closer to the present: In the early 1970s, a proposal to name the recently expanded University of Düsseldorf after the city's most famous son was turned down by the university authorities on grounds that for the faculty of medicine—the largest and oldest of the university—Heine's name has no particular relevance. But students settled the matter without the blessing of the authorities, unceremoniously and effectively, by sporting T-shirts imprinted *Heinrich Heine Universität*. Which other nineteenth-century literary figure could pass a similar test of "relevancy"? What if this were as much an expression of student protest as a proof of their appreciation of Heine's oeuvre: Heine once again was the center of a lively controversy, his figure a living myth.

The change of political climate after the end of World War II has brought about a drastic reversal in official German attitudes, and so the most recent version of a *Denkmalstreit* in Heine's city of birth was of quite a different sort. A Heine memorial, created by the sculptor Bert Gerresheim, was unveiled with considerable fanfare on the occasion of the one hundred and twenty-fifth anniversary of the poet's death, in a central location in Düsseldorf. In the meantime, city fathers were embarrassed by having to reject an offer of a second Heine statue by another sculptor. This time, however, it was not the worthiness of the subject that caused the objection but the compatibility of a sculptor who had enjoyed a healthy career under National Socialism.

Heine's one hundred and seventy-fifth birthday was made the occasion of an international Congress in Düsseldorf to which participants traveled from distant points of the globe. Characteristically, local students saw to it that their Heine not be smothered by the academic exercise. The result, in the words of one participant, was a blend of "scholarship, piety, and fracas."[26] A few weeks later, the German Democratic Republic held a session in Weimar when speakers from socialist countries praised their Heine. A Heine Institute has been established and an active Heine Society holds regular meetings in Düsseldorf and lately also in Hamburg. When a cultural exchange between West Germany and the Soviet Union was inaugurated in 1978, the first representative event was a display in Moscow of Heine memorabilia on loan from Germany.

Hand in hand with the public recognition and reception of Heine as a potent symbol went a lively increase of scholarly interest. First of all, his works, which were unobtainable in bookstores (thanks to the Nazi bonfires), had to be reissued. No less than twenty-four editions of his collected works—some partial, but many complete—have appeared on the market between 1960 and 1978, including two monumental critical editions, one in East Germany (Weimar) and one, still in progress, in West Germany. This avalanche of new editions is matched by an unparalleled flood of secondary literature. No other author, of any nationality and any period, has attracted so much scholarly attention within the last quarter century. (The present rate of production has been estimated as two hundred publications a year.)

Heine's true repatriation will, however, not be brought about merely through academic discussion and analysis but by his introduction into the school curricula of the Federal Republic. (In the German Democratic Republic he has long since been required reading.) To judge from the number of workshops, seminars, and various other "events" that focus on him, this repatriation is being promoted with the customary German thoroughness.[27] If he survives being treated as a classic and is not buried under the sheer weight of academic attention, Heine may be said to have returned to Germany at last!

Notes and References

Chapter One

1. "Der achzehnte Brumaire" (3:257):November 9, 1799, is the date of Napoleon's coup d'état when armed soldiers drove the legislators from the chambers. A new form of republic, the Consulate, was proclaimed, with Napoleon Bonaparte as first consul.
2. Remark to Fanny Lewald in *Gespräche mit Heine,* ed. H. H. Houben, (Frankfurt, 1926), p. 772; hereafter cited as Houben.
3. Friedrich Hirth, ed., *Heinrich Heine, Briefe,* 2 vols. (Mainz, 1950–51), 1:35, July 6, 1815; hereafter cited as Hirth, with volume and page number as well as date of correspondence.
4. Ibid., 1:5, October 27, 1816.
5. See Eberhard Galley, "Heine und die Burschenschaft. Ein Kapitel aus Heines politischem Werdegang zwischen 1819 und 1830" (*Heine Jahrbuch* 11 [1972]:66–95). The fraternity to which Heine briefly belonged had been newly founded and was euphemistically called "Allgemeinheit" (the universal community).
6. Manfred Windfuhr regards Heine as one of the first Young Hegelians, while J. L. Sammons and Ernst Loeb take at face value Heine's remark, "ehrlich gesagt, selten verstand ich ihn [Hegel]" ("Frankly, I rarely understood him"). Heine perpetuated this anecdote: "Als Hegel auf dem Todbette lag, sagte er: 'Nur einer hat mich verstanden,' aber gleich darauf fügte er verdriesslich hinzu: 'Und der hat mich auch nicht verstanden'" ("On his death bed, Hegel said, 'only one has understood me'—but he added grumpily, 'and he did not understand me either,'" (5:274). Dolf Sternberger maintains that Heine's belated perception of Hegel as a radical and subsequent rejection of him emerged only after he became acquainted with Marx and Ruge. See Manfred Windfuhr, "Heine und Hegel," in *Internationaler Heine-Kongress* (Düsseldorf, 1972), pp. 261–80; Jeffrey L. Sammons, *Heinrich Heine: The Elusive Poet* (New Haven, 1969); Ernst Loeb, *Heinrich Heine: Weltbild und geistige Gestalt* (Bonn, 1975), pp. 58–78; Dolf Sternberger, *Heinrich Heine und die Abschaffung der Sünde* (Hamburg, 1972); Hanna Spencer, "Heine: Between Hegel and Jehovah," in *Heinrich Heine, Dimensionen seines Wirkens* (Bonn, 1979), pp. 23–33.

151

7. An allusion to the fact that the Rhinelands came under Prussian jurisdiction in the wake of Napoleon's defeat, and Jewish rights of citizenship that had been granted under French rule were once again revoked.

8. J. L. Sammons, *Heinrich Heine: A Modern Biography* (Princeton, 1980), p. 138.

9. Compare *Das Junge Deutschland: Texte und Dokumente,* ed. Jost Hermand (Stuttgart: Reclam, 1966).

10. See E. M. Butler, *The Saint-Simonian Religion in Germany* (Cambridge: Cambridge University Press, 1926); (Reprint, New York: Howard Fertig, 1968.) Dolf Sternberger, *Heinrich Heine und die Abschaffung der Sünde* (Hamburg, 1972).

11. See chapter 4. Salomon Strauss was the husband of Jeannette Wohl, who had reason to feel insulted by Heine's cruel remarks about her relationship to Ludwig Börne and about her appearance. The duel took place in September, 1841, without serious injury to either participant. Such nineteenth-century duels have in more recent times been replaced by libel suits.

Chapter Two

1. In the context of *Buch der Lieder,* this poem is a love plaint. But it was originally written to commiserate with Heine's Düsseldorf school friend Gustav Friedrich von Unzer, who had been badly wounded at Waterloo and returned to the Lycée while still on crutches. See *Düsseldorfer Heine Ausgabe,* vol. 1, pt. 2, p. 686.

2. "Und was soll werden dein Weib und Kind? Edward, Edward . . . Die Welt ist gross, lass sie betteln drin, Mutter, Mutter!" Johann Gottfried Herder, *Stimmen der Völker in Liedern* (Leipzig: Reclam, 1968).

3. This is the only instance of such "irregularity" in "Lyrisches Intermezzo," where tetrametric lines usually alternate with trimetric ones.

4. *Düsseldorfer Heine Ausgabe,* vol. 1, pt. 2, pp. 812–14.

5. Gerhard Storz, *Heinrich Heines Lyrische Dichtung,* (Stuttgart: Klett, 1971), pp. 40, 48.

6. Manfred Windfuhr, "Heine und der Petrarkismus," in *Heinrich Heine,* ed. Helmut Koopmann (Darmstadt 1975), pp. 207–31.

7. Transl. by Howard Mumford Jones, in *Heine's Poem "The North Sea"* (Chicago, 1916).

8. Hirth, 1:329, October 30, 1827.

Chapter Three

1. Hirth, 1:196, March 4, 1825.

2. See Erich Loewenthal, *Studien zu Heines "Reisebildern"* (Berlin: Palaestra 138, 1922).

3. Matthew Arnold, "Heinrich Heine," in *Essays in Criticism*. (New York: Macmillan Co., 1924). (Reprint.)

4. Cf. Walter Dietze, *Junges Deutschland und deutsche Klassik* (Berlin: Rütten & Loening, 1957–62); Fritz Friedländer, "Heine und Goethe," in *Germanisch und Deutsch*, vol. 7 (Berlin, 1932); Gustav Karpeles, "Goethe und Heine," in *Heine und seine Zeitgenossen* (Berlin, 1888); Walter Wadepuhl, "Heines Verhältnis zu Goethe," in *Jahrbuch der Goethegesellschaft*, n.s. 18 (1956), pp. 121–31; Wolfgang Leppmann, *Goethe und die Deutschen* (Stuttgart, 1962), pp. 63–82; Sol Liptzin, *The English Legend of Heinrich Heine* (New York, 1954), pp. 59–81; Ulrich Maché, "Der junge Heine und Goethe," *Heine Jahrbuch* 4(1965): 42–47; Helmut Koopmann, "Heine in Weimar," *Zeitschrift für deutsche Philologie* 91 (1972); Hanna Spencer, "Heines Spiel mit Goethes Erbmantel," in *Dichter, Denker, Journalist*, (Bern, 1977), pp. 37–51.

5. Hirth, 1:34, December 29, 1821.

6. Ibid., 1:187, October 25, 1824.

7. Ibid., 1:210–11, May 26, 1825.

8. Cf. Günter Grass, *Die Blechtrommel* [The Tin Drum], (Darmstadt: Hermann Luchterhand, 1959).

9. A transparent allusion to the red cap of the Jacobins.

Chapter Four

1. See Leo Kreutzer, *Heine und der Kommunismus* (Göttingen: Vandenhoeck & Ruprecht, 1970); p. 24.

2. Mainly through the documentation provided by Babeuf's co-conspirator Philippe Buonarrotti. See *Conspiration pour l'Egalité dite de Babeuf* (Brussels, 1828); Kreutzer, p. 13.

3. See below, chaps. 6–7.

4. See Karl Marx, *Early Writing*, trans. and ed. T. B. Bottomore (New York: McGraw-Hill, 1964), p. 153. These economic and philosophical manuscripts—evidently written during the period when Marx and Heine met almost daily—were not published in Marx's lifetime. I am indebted to Professor F. M. Barnard for this information.

5. Louis XVI was beheaded on January 21, 1793.

6. Hirth, 2:309, 333, letters of April 12, 1839, and February 18, 1840.

7. "Ueber den Denunzianten" (5:388f.); Wolfgang Menzel's denunciation was suspected of having triggered the 1835 ban.

8. Hirth, 2:307, September, 1840.

9. Thomas Mann, *Gesammelte Werke* (Frankfurt: Fischer, 1960), 10:839.

10. For a fuller analysis, see Inge Rippmann, "Heines Denkschrift über Börne: Ein Doppelporträt," *Heine Jahrbuch* 12 (1973); 41–70; Hanna

Spencer, "Gipfel oder Tiefpunkt? Die Denkschrift für Ludwig Börne," in
Dichter, Denker, Journalist, pp. 101–49.
    11. "Shakespeares Mädchen und Frauen" (5:459ff.) and "Einleitung zu
Don Quichote" (5:406ff.).
    12. E. M. Butler, "Heine and the Saint-Simonians: The date of the
Letters from Heligoland," *Modern Language Review* 18 (1923):68–85; J. L.
Sammons, *Heinrich Heine: The Elusive Poet* (New Haven, 1969), pp. 257ff.;
Helmut Koopmann, *Heine Düsseldorfer Ausgabe,* vol. 2, *Ludwig Börne: Eine
Denkschrift,* pp. 455–58; Hanna Spencer, "Briefe aus Helgoland—
synchronische Chronik?" in *Dichter, Denker, Journalist,* pp. 118–29.

Chapter Five

    1. See E. M. Butler, *Tyranny of Greece over Germany* (Boston: Beacon
Press, 1958). Butler calls it the "first unequivocal recognition of the god
Dionysos in German literature"; "the first real response to the mysterious
ambiguous, fascinating deity" (pp. 11, 252).
    2. Cf. Karl Richter: "Heinrich Heine in Richard Wagners autobiog-
raphischen Schriften und in den Tagebüchern von Cosima Wagner," *Heine
Jahrbuch* 19 (1979): 209–17.
    3. See Barker Fairley, *Heinrich Heine* (Oxford, 1954), "Music and
Dance," pp. 24ff.
    4. In the *Wilde Jagd* -scene of *Atta Troll,* Diana is similarly presented.
    5. Michael Hamburger considers *Der Doktor Faust* to be Heine's most
profound work *(Reason and Energy* [London, 1957], p. 157).
    6. Abraxas is a cabalistic device. In Egk's ballet, it is the charm with
which Faust summons Mephistophela.

Chapter Six

    1. Cologne cathedral, started in 1248, was not finished until 1880;
Friedrich Wilhelm Schelling changed his philosophic views; and Friedrich
Wilhelm III never granted the constitution which he promised in 1813.
    2. The illustrious model is, of course, the *Walpurgisnacht* in Goethe's
Faust.
    3. See Kurt Weinberg, *Henri Heine: Romantique défroqué. Héraut du
symbolisme français* (New Haven, 1954); Oliver Boeck, *Heines Nachwirkung
und Heine-Parallelen in der französichen Dichtung* (Göppingen: Kümmerle,
1972).
    4. S. S. Prawer, *Tragic Satirist,* pp. 103–29; Heinrich Heine, *Atta Troll,
ein Sommernachtstraum—Deutschland, ein Wintermärchen,* ed. Barker Fairley
(Oxford, 1966).

5. Helmut Koopmann, "Heinrich Heine und die Politisierung des Mythos," in *Mythos und Mythologie in der Literatur des 19. Jahrhunderts* (Frankfurt: Vittorio Klostermann, 1979), pp. 141–58.

6. Nikolaus Becker wrote the popular "Rheinlied" (1840): "Sie sollen ihn nicht haben, den freien deutschen Rhein."

7. Cf. Franz Kafka, *The Penal Colony* (New York: Schocken, 1948).

8. Leo Kreutzer, *Heine und der Kommunismus* (Göttingen: Vandenhoeck & Ruprecht, 1970); Walther Victor, *Marx und Heine* (Berlin: Henschelverlag, 1970); Manfred Windfuhr, *Heinrich Heine: Revolution und Reflexion* (Stuttgart, 1969), pp. 264, 266.

9. See above, chapter 4.

Chapter Seven

1. For a summary listing of topics covered by Heine, see J. L. Sammons, *Heinrich Heine: A Modern Biography* (Princeton, 1979), pp. 323–30.

2. Some of these poems originated earlier; e.g., "Friedrike" is dated 1823.

3. In *Der Freimüthige,* ed. Willibald Alexis; reprinted in *Salon,* vol. 1.

4. Hirth, 2:277, August 23, 1838.

5. Dolf Sternberger, contains a charming analysis on pp. 104ff.

6. Laura Hofrichter made this struggle the central theme of her study *Heinrich Heine,* trans. Barker Fairley (Oxford, 1963).

7. What aggravated Heine's hurt and fury even more was the fact that this ruthless cousin Carl had come down with cholera in 1832 while visiting Paris and, for his sake, Heine did not join the exodus from the city.

8. R. R. Palmer and Joel Colton, *History of the Modern World* (New York: Alfred A. Knopf, 1965), pp. 472–74.

9. Hirth, 1:359, February 13, 1852.

10. Ibid., 1:133, April 12, 1848.

11. For reasons that are not quite clear, Campe had taken offense and for three years did not reply to Heine's letters.

12. Cf. Hermann J. Weigand, "Heine's Return to God," *Modern Philology* 18 (1920): 309–42; William Rose, *Heinrich Heine* (Oxford, 1956), pp. 94–136; J. L. Sammons, *The Elusive Poet* (New Haven, 1969), pp. 349f.; Dolf Sternberger, *Heinrich Heine und die Abschaffung der Sünde* (Hamburg, 1972); Hartmut Kircher, *Heinrich Heine und das Judentum* (Bonn: Bouvier, 1973); Ludwig Rosenthal, *Heinrich Heine als Jude* (Frankfurt, 1973); Wilhelm Gössmann, "Die theologische Revision Heines in der Spätzeit," and Louis Cuby, "Die theologische Revision in Heines Spätzeit," both in *Heine Studien,* Internationaler Heine-Kongress (Düsseldorf, 1972), pp. 320–42; Ernst Simon, "Heines Stellung zum Judentum," ibid., pp. 318f;

Peter Heinegg, "Heine's Conversion and the Critics," *German Life and Letters* 30 (1976–77): 45–55; Ernst Loeb, *Heinrich Heine, Weltbild und geistige Gestalt* (Bonn, 1975), pp. 58–78; Hanna Spencer, "Heine: Between Hegel und Jehovah," in *Heinrich Heine: Dimensionen seines Wirkens* (Bonn, 1979), pp. 23–33.

13. Houben, p. 63.

14. "In der Kunst bin ich Supernaturalist. Ich glaube, dass (dem Künstler) . . . die bedeutendsten Typen, als eingeborene Symbolik eingeborner Ideen, gleichsam in der Seele geoffenbart werden" (4:316). The analogy of artistic creativity and divine creation is the theme of "Schöpfungslieder" [Songs of Creation], a group within *Neue Gedichte* (1:266f.).

15. Hirth, 1:194f., January 25, 1850.

16. Ibid., 1:147, June 23, 1848.

17. Houben, p. 656.

18. The chapter "The Poet's Workshop" in S. S. Prawer's *The Tragic Satirist* includes several such examples and perceptively analyzes them (pp. 209ff.).

19. "Ich habe gearbeitet, ordentlich gearbeitet an meinen Versen" (Houben, p. 743).

20. Hirth, 1:228, September 28, 1850.

21. Heine's source may have been a story in Stendhal's *De L'Amour* (1822), chap. 53.

22. Cf. Franz Kafka, "Up in the Gallery," in *The Penal Colony* (New York: Schocken, 1948).

23. Heine, 2:30; Goethe, Werke, 50 vols. (*Weimar: H. Böhlau, 1887–1912*), 1:230.

24. "Schlaf, Kindchen, schlaf! Der Vater hüt' die Schaf', / die Mutter schüttelt's Bäumelein, / fällt herab ein Träumelein, / schlaf, Kindchen, schlaf!"

25. The connotation of *Köhlerglaube* as simple (blind) faith goes back to Luther's time.

26. Cf. chapter 6. Bertolt Brecht made similar use of this lullaby by paraphrasing it in *Mutter Courage*: "Eia popeia was raschelt im Stroh? Nachbars Bälg greinen und meine sind froh" (Brecht, *Stücke* [Frankfurt: Suhrkamp, 1957]), 7:202.

27. Campe informed Heine in 1847 that a reading of his "Weberlied" "put a poor devil in jail" (Hirth, 2:61). And even fifty years later, in the Germany of Wilhelm II, the reprinting of Heine's song was punishable with a six-months prison term. See H. Schwab-Felisch, *Hauptmann: Die Weber. Dichtung und Wirklichkeit* (Frankfurt: Ullstein, 1959), p. 152.

28. Ibid., p. 152.

29. Cf. Karl-Heinz Hahn, "Die Wanderratten" (1963) in *Heinrich Heine,* ed. Helmut Koopmann (Darmstadt: Wissenschaftliche Buchgemeinschaft, 1975), pp. 117–32.

30. See *Les derniers Jours de H. Heine* (Paris: Calman Levy, 1884). For fuller information on Camille Selden, see Sammons, *A Modern Biography,* pp. 341f.

Chapter Eight

1. Cf. K. H. Fingerhut, *Standortbestimmungen* (Hildesheim, 1971).

2. To Friedrich Wilhelm Rogge in 1836: "Aber Sie glauben nicht, was mir dieser Stil für Mühe und Arbeit macht" (Houben, p. 301).

3. Hirth, 1:xix (introduction): "Alle französischen Historiker, von Thureau-Dangin bis Banville, sehen in Heine den zuverlässigsten Beobachter dieser Periode der französischen Geschichte."

4. Kurt Weinberg, "Heine and French Poetry," *Yale French Studies,* no. 6 (1950), pp. 45–52; and Weinberg, *Henri Heine: Romantique défroqué*"; see also Oliver Boeck.

5. Matthew Arnold, "Heinrich Heine," in *Essays in Criticism* (1849; reprint, New York: Macmillan, 1924), pp. 156–93; George Eliot, "German Wit: Heinrich Heine," in *Essays and Leaves from a Note-Book* (New York: Nelson, 1906).

6. See Sol Liptzin, *The English Legend of Heinrich Heine* (New York, 1954).

7. See A. E. Housman's *Shropshire Lad.* Cf. Herman Salinger, "Housman's *Last Poems,* XXX and Heine's *Lyrisches Intermezzo,* 62," *Modern Language Notes* 54 (1939): 288–90.

8. For instance, Stuart Atkins, Carl Brinitzer, E. M. Butler, Barker Fairley, Ernst Feise, Laura Hofrichter, Michael Hamburger, Sol Liptzin, Ernst Loeb, Heinz Politzer, S. S. Prawer, Nigel Reeves, William Rose, J. L. Sammons, A. I. Sandor, Meno Spann, Hanna Spencer, J. P. Stern, Israel Tabak, Hermann Weigand, Kurt Weinberg—the list could be continued.

9. Ernst Loeb, p. 80.

10. Sol Liptzin, p. 121.

11. Hans Kaufmann, *Heine, Werke und Briefe,* 10:103f.

12. Alexander Schweickert, *Heinrich Heines Einflüsse auf die deutsche Lyrik 1830–1900* (Bonn, 1969).

13. Heine served Sigmund Freud as his main example for the study on wit and its relation to the unconscious; see *Jokes and their Relation to the Unconscious,* (New York: Norton, 1960). Anyone familiar with Heine's views will be assailed by a sense of déjà vu when reading Freud's essays on *Moses and Monotheism* (London: Hogarth Press, 1939). With regard to Heine and the

"uncanny" (as interpreted by Freud), see Kurt Weinberg, "Die Entsub-
limierung des Unheimlichen im Werk Heines," in *Heinrich Heine, Dimensionen seines Wirkens* (Bonn, 1979). As for Carl Gustav Jung, his doctoral
dissertation dealt with female prototypes in Heine's work. See Gustav Jung,
Die Darstellung des Weibes in Heines Werken (Leipzig: F. S. Krauss, 1920);
Jung, "Der Erotiker Heinrich Heine," *Zeitschrift für Sexualwissenschaft* 11
(1924): 113–28.

14. The discovery of this intellectual link is of relatively recent origin,
partly because it seemed difficult to recognize an affinity between two men
whose spheres of influence at a first glance seemed so disparate. See Hanna
Spencer, "Heine and Nietzsche," *Heine Jahrbuch* 11 (1972): 126–161.

15. "Zu Heines Gedächtnis," *Veröffentlichungen der Dramatischen
Gesellschaft*, no. 2, Bonn, December 16, 1899.

16. Helmut Koopmann, "Heinrich Heine in Deutschland," *Heinrich
Heine*, ed. Koopmann (Darmstadt: Wissenschaftliche Buchgemeinschaft,
1975).

17. George L. Mosse, *The Crisis of German Ideology: Intellectual Origins of
the Third Reich* (New York: Universal Library, 1964), p. 28.

18. Hans Mayer, "Die Ausnahme Heinrich Heine," in *Heinrich Heine
Werke*, 4 vols. (Frankfurt: Insel Verlag, 1968), 1:7–26.

19. Friedrich Nietzsche, *Gesammelte Werke*, 23 vols. (Munich: Musarion,
1920–29), 17:121, 103; 15:217; 16:404.

20. Walter Muschg, *Tragische Literaturgeschichte* (Bern: Francke, 1957),
pp. 85, 269.

21. Karl Kraus, "Heine und die Folgen," in *Werke* (Munich: Koesel,
1960), 8:188–213. The article originally appeared in 1910.

22. Apart from the inherent unfairness of a critique which would burden
the model with the transgressions of the imitators, the basis for—and the
fallacy of—the Kraus attack has been probed and exposed in a study by
Mechthild Borries, *Ein Angriff auf Heinrich Heine, Kritische Betrachtungen zu
Karl Kraus* (Stuttgart: Kohlhammer, 1971). See also Bernd Kämmerling,
"Die wahre Richtung des Angriffs: Über Karl Kraus': 'Heine und die
Folgen,'" *Heine Jahrbuch* 11 (1972): 162–169.

23. Stefan Zweig, *Briefe an Freunde*, ed. Richard Friedenthal (Frankfurt,
1978), pp. 91–92. I am indebted to my colleague Günter Hess for this
reference.

24. See Gerhard Storz, *Heinrich Heines lyrische Dichtung* (Stuttgart: Klett,
1971), p. 5.

25. Wilhelm Gössmann, ed. *Geständnisse: Heine im Gedächtnis heutiger
Autoren,* (Düsseldorf, 1972).

26. J. L. Sammons, in *English Language Notes,* supp. (1978).

27. The list of lectures, revues, recitals, exhibits, radio and television programs, seminars, etc., that have Heine as their subject takes up ten printed pages. See "Heine-Chronik 1977–78," comp. Inge Hermstrüwer, *Heine Jahrbuch* 11 (1979): 281–91.

Selected Bibliography

PRIMARY SOURCES

1. German editions

Sämtliche Werke. Edited by Ernst Elster. 7 vols. Leipzig: Bibliographisches Institut, 1887–90.

Werke und Briefe. Edited by Hans Kaufmann. 10 vols. Berlin: Aufbau Verlag, 1961–64. The first comprehensive edition since the onset of the post-war Heine interest. Includes a selection of letters and is supplied with an index in volume 10. These features and the fact that it is printed in Roman type recommended its use for my study—rather than the Elster edition.

Historisch-kritische Gesamtausgabe der Werke. Düsseldorfer Ausgabe. Edited by Manfred Windfuhr et al. Hamburg: Hoffmann und Campe, 1973–.

Heinrich Heine Säkularausgabe. Edited by Nationale Forschungs-und Gedenkstätten der klassischen deutschen Literatur in Weimar and Centre National de la Recherche Scientifique in Paris. Berlin and Paris: Akademie-Verlag and Editions du CNRS, 1970–1980.

For other editions see Jeffrey L. Sammons, "Current Heine Editions," *German Quarterly* 44 (1971): 628–42.

2. English translations

Lyric Poems and Ballads. Translated by Ernst Feise. Pittsburgh: University of Pittsburgh Press, 1961. A bilingual anthology, with a free translation in poetic form.

Heine. Edited and translated by Peter Branscombe. Harmondsworth: Penguin Books, 1967. A generous anthology of the original poems, followed by a literal prose translation.

Heine's Poem "The North Sea." Translated by Howard Mumford Jones. Chicago: Open Court Publishing Co., 1916. The translator attempts to imitate the original rhythms.

Selected Works. Translated by Helen M. Mustard and Max Knight. New York: Vintage Books, 1973.

A Biographical Anthology. Edited by Hugo Bieber and translated by Moses Hadas. Philadelphia: Jewish Publication Society of America, 1959.

The Poetry and Prose. Edited by Frederic Ewen and translated by Louis Untermeyer, Frederic Ewen et al. New York: Citadel Press, 1948.

Bittersweet Poems of Heinrich Heine. Translated by Joseph Auslander. Mount Vernon, N. Y.: Peter Pauper Press, 1956.

Untermeyer, Louis. *Heinrich Heine: Paradox and Poet. The Poems.* New York: Harcourt, Brace, 1937. The poet Untermeyer freely translates a selection of Heine poems.

3. English bibliography

Arnold, Armin. *Heine in England and America: A Bibliographical Checklist.* Introduction by William Rose. London: Linden Press, 1959.

4. Biographical documents

Briefe. Edited by Friedrich Hirth. 2 vols. Mainz: Kupferberg, 1950–51.

Gespräche mit Heine. Edited by H. H. Houben. Frankfurt: Rütten & Loening, 1926. These conversations with Heine have been incorporated in a more recent and more comprehensive compilation:

Begegnungen mit Heine, in Fortführung von H. H. Houben's "Gespräche mit Heine." Edited by Michael Werner. 2 vols. Hamburg: Hoffmann and Campe, 1973.

Heinrich Heine: Dichter über ihre Dichtungen. Edited by Norbert Altenhofer. 3 vols. Munich: Heimeran, 1971. The author's own references to his works are listed. Includes a very useful index.

Heinrich Heine, Gespräche, Briefe, Tagebücher, Berichte seiner Zeitgenossen. Edited by Hugo Bieber. Berlin: Weltverlag, 1926.

Heinrich Heine: Chronik seines Lebens und Werkes. Edited by Fritz Mende. Berlin: Akademie-Verlag, 1970. This compendium chronicles Heine's activities month by month and, where possible, day by day, based on documentary evidence.

SECONDARY SOURCES

Literature about Heine is copious. But he has been very well served by bibliographers: Gottfried Wilhelm and Eberhard Galley, *Heine Bibliographie* (Weimar: Arion Verlag, 1960), 2 vols. (to 1953), and Siegfried Seifert, *Heine-Bibliographie 1954–1964* (Berlin and Weimar: Aufbau-Verlag, 1968), have listed nine thousand items of primary and secondary materials. Since 1962 the bibliography has been continued annually in the *Heine-Jahrbuch*. A very useful annotated bibliography has been published since my manuscript went into print: Jeffrey L. Sammons. *Heinrich Heine. A Selected Critical Bibliography of Secondary Literature, 1956–1980.* New York and London: Garland Publishing Inc., 1982.

Brinitzer, Carl. *H. Heine. Roman seines Lebens.* Hamburg: Hoffmann und Campe, 1960. An account of Heine's life, based in part on the poet's own testimony. Written in a lively style, this book is not meant to be a scholarly study but a biographical novel.

Brod, Max. *Heinrich Heine: The Artist in Revolt.* London: Valentine, Mitchell, 1956. This English version of an earlier (1934) biographical study emphasizes Heine's Jewishness. This book is rewarding for its penetrating insights and the author's own mature wisdom.

Butler, E. M. *Heinrich Heine: A Biography.* London: Hogarth Press, 1956. This colorful account of Heine's life is important because it draws attention to the Saint-Simonian influences upon him. It also points out his "discovery" of the dionysian experience for German literature. Professor Butler writes vividly and engagingly. Her presentation of the poet's suffering in his mattress grave is memorable.

Fairley, Barker. *Heinrich Heine: An Interpretation.* Oxford: Clarendon Press, 1954. Appearing near the beginning of the recent Heine renaissance, this study broke new ground in Heine research. Rather than paying attention to Heine's personality, the author turned to the texts themselves and explored them with regard to the most pervasive images. Barker Fairley's lucid, economical prose is a pleasure to read.

Fingerhut, Karl-Heinz. *Standortbestimmungen: Vier Untersuchungen zu Heinrich Heine.* Heidenheim: Heidenheimer Verlagsanstalt, 1973. This interesting and useful book contains four essays, each of which deals with an apparent dichotomy in Heine's position. In each case the author explains the seeming contradiction by demonstrating a change in context; that is to say, he shows that the changed viewpoint is due to a changed point of view, in the original, literal sense of the term (*Standort*).

Galley, Eberhard. *Heinrich Heine: Lebensbericht mit Bildern und Dokumenten.* Kassel: Wenderoth, 1973. A well illustrated and documented chronicle of Heine's life, produced by the founder and first editor of the *Heine Jahrbuch,* curator for many years of the Heine Archive in Düsseldorf and foremost bibliographer of Heine's works.

Gössmann, Wilhelm, ed. *Geständnisse: Heine im Bewusstsein heutiger Autoren.* Düsseldorf: Droste, 1972. Contemporary authors were asked to record what reactions Heine's image and work evoked in them. This volume contains about ninety very diverse and intriguing responses.

Hamburger, Michael. "Heinrich Heine." In: *Contraries: Studies in German Literature,* pp. 240–69. New York: Dutton, 1970.

Hermand, Jost. *Der frühe Heine: Ein Kommentar zu den "Reisebildern".* Munich: Winkler, 1976. A leading expert comments on Heine's Travel Sketches, with special emphasis on their socio-political critique. My pertinent chapter draws on Professor Hermand's findings.

Hofrichter, Laura. *Heinrich Heine.* Translated by Barker Fairley. Oxford: Clarendon Press, 1963. Barker Fairley's superb translation of this imaginative study appeared before the German (posthumously published) original became available. Laura Hofrichter's basic theme is the poet's prolonged but eventually successful struggle to free himself from the spell and constraints of the folksong model which had so effectively dominated his early verse.

Kaufmann, Hans. *Heinrich Heine: Geistige Entwicklung und künstlerisches Werk.* Berlin and Weimar: Aufbau-Verlag, 1967. An important and interesting introduction to Heine's mind and work by the leading East German Heine scholar. It goes without saying that the author discusses at length Heine's position within the socialist tradition.

Koopmann, Helmut, ed. *Heinrich Heine.* Darmstadt: Wissenschaftliche Buchgemeinschft, 1975. A selection of interesting essays on Heine by various authors.

Kurz, Paul Konrad. *Künstler, Tribun, Apostel: Heinrich Heines Auffassung vom Beruf des Dichters.* Munich: Fink, 1967. A thorough, scholarly, informative study examines Heine's self-understanding as artist.

Liptzin, Sol. *The English Legend of Heinrich Heine.* New York: Bloch, 1954. As the title indicates, this book deals with Heine's legendary fame in England. It traces its origins and describes its various stages and aspects. Stimulating and useful.

Loeb, Ernst. *Heinrich Heine: Weltbild und geistige Gestalt.* Bonn: Bouvier, 1975. Four perceptive essays deal with important problems in Heine's view of the world and of himself, notably the dichotomy of truth and beauty, the dilemma of engagement and distance, and his religious thought and feeling. One essay discusses Heine's view of Luther and of Napoleon. Professor Loeb writes with a flair and wit that serves his subject well.

Marcuse, Ludwig. *A Life Between Love and Hate.* New York: Farrar & Rinehart, 1933. In revised form, this book appeared again in 1951 and, once more revised and enlarged, as *Heine: Melancholiker, Streiter in Marx, Epikureer.* Rotenburg ob der Tauber: Peter, Holstein, 1970. The historical and sociological background is emphasized. Anything but a detached scholarly study, this account demonstrates the personal involvement and identification that Heine has been able to elicit a century after his death. A worthwhile and intriguing book, rich in valuable insights.

Mayer, Hans. "Heinrich Heine, German Ideology, and German Ideologists." *New German Critique* 1, no. 1 (1973):2–18.

Prawer, S. S. *Heine: Buch der Lieder.* London: Edward Arnold, 1960.

————. *Heine the Tragic Satirist: A Study of the Later Poetry 1827–1856.* Cambridge: Cambridge University Press, 1961. Brilliant, exquisitely sensitive and imaginative interpretations. These two volumes deal with Heine's entire poetic oeuvre. I am profoundly indebted to Professor Prawer's research.

Reeves, Nigel. *Heinrich Heine: Poetry and Politics.* Oxford: Oxford University Press, 1974.

Rose, William. *The Early Love Poetry of Heinrich Heine: An Enquiry into Poetic Inspiration.* Oxford: Clarendon Press, 1962.

————. *Heinrich Heine: Two Studies of his Thought and Feeling.* Oxford: Clarendon Press, 1956. In the first mentioned volume, the author investigates—and seriously questions—to what extent Heine's love poetry may be taken at face value, as part of an autobiographical confession. The second volume contains excellent explorations of Heine's political and social attitude, and of his Jewish feeling.

Rosenthal, Ludwig. *Heinrich Heine als Jude.* Frankfurt am Main and Berlin: Ullstein, 1973. A knowledgeable discussion of the Jewish influences on Heine. To paraphrase Eberhard Galley's introductory remarks to the book, the author's familiarity with all aspects of Jewish lore, customs, sociological background, etc., makes a significant contribution to the elucidation of many aspects in Heine's life and work.

Sammons, Jeffrey L. *Heinrich Heine: The Elusive Poet.* New Haven: Yale University Press, 1969. Throughout this detailed analysis of Heine's writings, the author separates the poetic persona from the poet's empirical self.

————. *Heinrich Heine: A Modern Biography.* Princeton: Princeton University Press, 1979. A painstakingly critical, analytical study, intent on shedding light on Heine's personage which seems as elusive as it is controversial. The poet emerges as a beleaguered individual, perpetually at odds with his surroundings. The designation "modern" in the subtitle seems to refer to the fact that this is a fully documented biography—in contrast to the many colorful yet highly subjective accounts which have appeared from time to time—and that the author, a leading expert whose knowledgeability on Heine and Heine research is awesome, was able to utilize the wealth of fresh information and insights supplied by recent research. He is scrupulously cautious—at times, one feels, excessively so—in distrusting Heine's own evidence. The final chapter gives a thoughtful, balanced overview of Heine's posthumous reception in Germany. The book contains an excellent (select) bibliography.

Sandor, A. I. *The Exile of Gods: Interpretation of a Theme, a Theory and a Technique in the Work of Heinrich Heine.* The Hague: Mouton, 1967.

Schweickert, Alexander. *Heinrich Heines Einflüsse auf die deutsche Lyrik 1830–1900.* Bonn: Bouvier, 1969. As promised in the title, this study traces Heine's influence on nineteenth-century German poetry.

Spann, Meno. *Heine.* London: Bowes and Bowes, 1966. A lively, brief introduction to the "phenomenon" Heine and his work.

Spencer, Hanna. *Dichter, Denker, Journalist:* Studien zum Werk Heinrich Heines. Bern, Frankfurt and Las Vegas: Lang, 1977. Six essays on Heine. One of these lists striking congruences in the works of Heine and Nietzsche.

———— and Raymond Immerwahr, ed.: *Heinrich Heine, Dimensionen seines Wirkens.* Bonn: Bouvier, 1979. Contains the papers presented on occasion of the international Heine Symposium held at London, Ontario.

Stern, J. P. "History and Prophecy: Heine." In *Re-Interpretations: Seven Studies in Nineteenth-Century German Literature.* New York: Basic Books, 1964.

Sternberger, Dolf. *Heinrich Heine und die Abschaffung der Sünde* [Heinrich Heine and the abolition of sin]. Düsseldorf: Claassen, 1972. 2d ed. Frankfurt am Main: Suhrkamp, 1976. The promise of this intriguing title is kept in this brilliant, penetrating presentation of Heine's religious thought. Emphasis rests on the Saint-Simonian influences. Written in an elegant and witty style, this is a very sophisticated, engaging book. A second edition (in paperback) was expanded to include the author's reply to scholars who had commented on his study: an example of stimulating scholarly dialogue.

Weinberg, Kurt. *Henri Heine: "Romantique défroqué." Héraut du symbolisme français.* New Haven and Paris: Yale University Press, 1954. This imaginative presentation of Heine as a precursor of French symbolism made an important contribution to the revaluation of Heine's position in European intellectual history. Professor Weinberg writes elegant prose, and seems equally at ease in French, English, and German.

Windfuhr, Manfred. *Heinrich Heine: Revolution und Reflexion.* Stuttgart: Metzler, 1969. A thorough and knowledgeable chronicle of Heine's life and work, by an author who has since become editor-in-chief of the monumental critical Heine edition which is presently being produced at Düsseldorf. Professor Windfuhr's presentation may seem somewhat sober but conversely, it has the advantage of being clear and easy to read.

—————, ed. *Internationaler Heine Kongress 1972: Referate und Diskussionen.* Hamburg: Hoffmann und Campe, 1973.

Heine Jahrbuch. Hamburg: Hoffmann und Campe, 1962–.

Index

Adam, Adolphe, 71
Alexis, Willibald (Wilhelm Här-
ing), 155n3
Anti-Semitism, 1, 8, 27, 41, 62, 66,
69, 77, 145, 147
Aristophanes, 114
Arminius (Hermann), 87
Arnold, Matthew, 33, 144, 153n3,
157n5
Artistic autonomy, 35, 63, 73, 127,
128
Ascher, Saul, 33
Atkins, Stuart, 157n8
Augsburg Allgemeine Zeitung, 44, 45,
94, 109, 110, 136

Babeuf, Gracchus (François Noêl),
46, 92, 153n2
Balzac, Honoré de, 10
Barnard, F.M., 153n4
Baudelaire, Charles, 144
Becker, Nikolaus, 85, 155n6
Bellini, Vincenzo, 10
Benn, Gottfried, 126
Berlioz, Louis Hector, 10
Bible, 15, *49, 50,* 54, 59, 60, 68,
123, 131, 145
Boeck, Oliver, 154n3, 157n4
Börne, Ludwig, 7, 11, 35, 55–63,
64, 77, 152n11

Borries, Mechthild, 158n22
Bottomore, T.B., 153n4
Brecht, Bertolt, 156n26
Brentano, Clemens, 20
Brinitzer, Carl, 157n8
Burns, Robert, 20
Butler, E.M., 152n10, 154n1,
154n12, 157n8
Byron, George Gordon Noel, Lord,
7, 14, 15, 35, 126

Caesar, Gaius Julius, 61
Campe, Julius, (Hoffmann und
Campe), 4, 6, 12, 29, 30, 56, 64,
79, 109, 115, 155n11, 156n27
Cartesius, Renatus (René Des-
cartes), 76
Cervantes Saavedra, Miguel de, 57
Chamisso, Adelbert, 53
Charlemagne (Carolus Magnus), 85
Charles I, King of England, 126
Charles V, King of Spain, German
Emperor, 43
Charles X, King of France, 9
Chopin, Fréderic, 10
Christiani, Rudolf, (married Heine's
cousin Charlotte), 34
Colton, Joel, 155n8
Communism, 45, 46, 47, 92, 113,
136–38, 153n1

Cotta von Cottendorf, Johann Friedrich von, 7, 44, 45
Cromwell, Oliver, 126
Cuby, Louis, 155n12
Cui, César, 71

Danton, Georges Jacques, 45
Delacroix, Eugène, 45
Demonization, 53–55, 119
Death of God, 15, 38, 49–51, 68, 110, 111, 126, 145
Denkmalstreit, 146, 147, 149
Dietze, Walter, 153n4
Dionysus, 65, 145, 154n1
Doppelgänger, 25, 26, 86, 88
Dream, 23, 33, 38, 68, 88, 97, 106, 107, 146
Dumas, Alexandre, 10

Egk, Werner, 72, 154n6
Eichendorff, Joseph von, 20
Eliot, George, 144, 157n5
Elisabeth, Empress of Austria, 146
Emancipation, 1, 10, 35, 39, 41, 45, 49, 57, 59, 61, 69, 82, 111, 113
Enfantin, Barthélemy Prosper ("Père Enfantin"), 6, 9, 47
Engels, Friedrich, 134
English, The, 41, 42, 65, 66, 144, 145

Fairley, Barker, 154n3, 154n4, 155n6, 157n8
Feise, Ernst, 157n8
Feuerbach, Ludwig, 77
Fichte, Johann Gottlieb, 51, 68
Fingerhut, K.H., 157n1
Fiore, Joachim de, 100
Flying Dutchman, Tale of the, 69
Folksong, 12, 20, 27, 28, 54, 80, 95, 101

Frederick William III, King of Prussia, 154n1
Frederick William IV, King of Prussia, 104, 105
Freiligrath, Ferdinand, 101
Freud, Sigmund, 48, 63, 68, 145, 157n13
Friedenthal, Richard, 158n23
Friedländer, Fritz, 153n4

Galley, Eberhard, 151n5
Gans, Eduard, 5
Gautier, Théophile, 10
Gerresheim, Bert, 149
Goethe, Johann Wolfgang, 2, 5, 8, 10, 18, 20, 25, 28, 30 (*Werther*), 34, 35, 38, 39, 52, 53, 59, 63, 71, 72, 78, 80, 99, 110, 123, 145, 153n4, 154n2
Gössmann, Wilhelm, 155n12, 158n25
Gottsched, Johann Christoph, 45
Grass, Günter, 63, 89, 153n8
Grimm, Gottlieb Christian, 6
Grimm, Jakob, 7
Grimm, Ludwig Emil, 7
Grimm, Wilhelm, 7
Gutzkow, Karl, 64, 99, 142

Hahn, Karl-Heinz, 157n29
Haller, Albrecht von, 27
Hamburger, Michael, 154n5, 157n8
Hauff, Wilhelm, 123
Hauptmann, Gerhart, 134
Hegel, Georg Wilhelm Friedrich, 5, 6, 31, 36, 37, 48, 52, 102, 103, 112, 113, 151n6
Heine, Amalie (cousin Molly), married Jonathan Friedländer, 3
Heine, Betty (née van Geldern, Heinrich's mother), 2, 78, 91, 106, 108

Heine, Carl (cousin), 107, 155n7
Heine, Charlotte (sister), 2
Heine, Gustav (brother), 2
Heine, Heinrich

WORKS: POETRY
(Untitled poems are identifed by
their first line.)
"Adam der Erste", 103, 104
"Affrontenburg", 133
"Almansor", 27
"Anfangs wollt ich fast verza-
gen", 13
"Angelique", 98
"Apollogott, Der", 119–22
"Asra, Der", 118
Atta Troll. Ein Sommernachtstraum,
71, 73–78,92, 93, 101, 154n4
"Auf diesem Felsen bauen wir",
("Seraphine"), 99–101
"Aus der Harzreise", 12
"Belsazar", 14, 15
"Bergidylle", 6, 27
"Bimini", 140
Buch der Lieder, 6, 12–29, 47, 94,
101, 119, 145, 152n1
"Clarisse", 98
"Das Fräulein stand am Meere",
97, 98
"Das Meer erglänzte weit
hinaus", 25
"Denk ich an Deutschland in der
Nacht" ("Nachtgedanken"),
105–107, 145
Deutschland. Ein Wintermärchen,
78–93, 94, 107, 126
"Diana", 98
"Dichter Firdusi, Der", 118, 119
"Die Jahre kommen und gehen",
23, 24
"Die Lotosblume ängstigt, 19, 20

"Die Söhne des Glückes beneid
ich nicht", 114
"Disputation", 128
"Doktrin", 102
"Donna Clara", 27
"Ein Fichtenbaum steht einsam",
18, 19
"Ein Jüngling liebt ein Mäd-
chen", 24
"Emma", 98
"Es ragt ins Meer der Runens-
tein", 95, 96
"Fragen", 28, 29
"Friedrike", 98, 155n2
"Für die Mouche", 139, 140
"Gedächtnisfeier", 129–31
Gedichte, 30, 34
Gedichte 1853/1854, 115, 131
"Goldne Kalb, Das", 123
"Gotter Griechenlands, Die" 28
"Götterdämmerung", 27, 69
"Grenadiere, Die", 13
"Hebräische Melodien", 126
"Heimkehr, Die", 12, 15, 20, 25,
27, 86
"Historien", 115, 119–26
"Hortense", 98
"Ich hatte einst ein schönes Vat-
erland", 96, 97
"Ich weiss nicht, was soll es be-
deuten" ("Loreley"), 20–22
"Im wunderschönen Monat Mai"
("Intermezzo" No 1) 16–18
"Jehuda Ben Halevy", 126
"Junge Leiden", 12
"Kaiser von China, Der", 104
"Karl I", 124–26
"Katherina", 98
"Lamentationen", 128
"Lass die heil'gen Parabolen",
131, 132
"Lazarus", 128, 131–33, 138, 139

"Leise zieht durch mein Gemüt", 95
"Loreley", 20–22
"Lyrisches Intermezzo", 12, 15, 23, 24, 70, 152n3
"Maria Antoinette", 117
"Marie", 98
"Mich locken nicht die Himmelsauen", 133
"Nachtgedanken", 105–107, 145, ("Denk ich an Deutschland")
"Nächtliche Fahrt", 118, 123
Neue Gedichte, 79, 94–107, 119, 156n14
"Neuer Frühling", 94
"Die Nordsee", 12, 27–30, 101
"Pfalzgräfin Jutta", 117, 124
"Pomare", 118, 123
"Prinzessin Sabbat", 126
"Rhampsenit", 115–17
"Romanzen", 94
Romanzero, 112, 114–28
"Rückschau", 129
"Salomo", 139
"Schelm von Bergen", 117
"Schlesischen Weber, Die", 133–36, 156n27
"Schöpfungslieder", 156n14
"Seraphine", 98–101
"Sklavenschiff, Das", 133
"Still ist die Nacht, es ruhen die Gassen", 25, 26
"Tannhäuser", 54, 101
"Teurer Freund! Was soll es nützen", 27
"Verschiedene", 94, 98, 99
"Vitziputzli", 118, 119
"Walküren", 117
"Wallfahrt nach Kevlaar, Die", 27

"Wanderratten, Die", 136–38
"Weisse Elefant, Der", 117
Wintermächen. See: Deutschland. Ein Wintermärchen
"Yolante", 98
"Zeitgedichte", 94, 101–107
"Zur Ollea", 94

WORKS: PROSE
Aus den Memoiren des Herrn von Schnabelewopski, 67–69
"Bäder von Lucca, Die", 39, 40, 41
"Berichtigung", 110
Denkschrift für Ludwig Börne, 48, 55–63, 73, 74, 92, 94, 101
"Einleitung zu Don Quichote", 57, 154n11
"Elementargeister", 54, 55, 64, 69, 71
"Englische Fragmente", 41–43
Florentinische Nächte, 65, 71
"Französische Maler", 45
"Französische Zustände", 45, 62
Geschichte der Religion und Philosophie in Deutschland, Die, 47–52, 64
"Geständnisse", 115
"Götter im Exil, Die", 55
Harzreise, Die, 6, 32–35, 36, 39
Ideen–Das Buch LeGrand, 37–39
Ludwig Börne. See: Denkschrift für Ludwig Börne
Lutetia, 45, 47, 94
"Nordsee III, Die", 35–37, 69
Rabbi von Bacharach, Der, 66, 67
"Reise von München nach Genua", 39, 40
Reisebilder, 6, 7, 8, 30, 31–43, 44, 71

Romantische Schule, Die, 47, 52, 53, 64, 69
Salon, Der, 44, 67, 143, 155n3
"Shakespeares Mädchen und Frauen", 57, 154n11
"Stadt Lucca, Die", 39, 40
"Uber die französische Bühne",45
Vermischte Schriften, 115

WORKS: DRAMA and BALLET
Almansor, 30, 34, 70, 71
Doktor Faust, Der, 71, 72, 154n5
Göttin Diana, Die, 71
William Ratcliff, 30, 34, 70, 71

Heine, Mathilde (née Eugenie Crescencia Mirat, wife), 10, 11, 54, 79, 129–31
Heine, Maximilian (brother), 2, 7
Heine, Salomon (uncle), 3, 4, 8, 9, 11, 78, 107, 119
Heine, Samson (father), 2, 8
Heine, Therese (cousin), married Adolf Halle, 3
Heinegg, Peter, 155n12
Hellenism. *See* Sensualism and Spiritualism
Herder, Johann Gottfried, 59, 152n2
Hermand, Jost, 152n9
Hermstrüwer, Inge, 159n27
Herodotus, 115
Herwegh, Georg, 101
Hess, Günter, 158n23
Hillebrand, Karl, 115
Hitler, Adolf, 20, 145, 146, 147
Hoffmann und Campe. *See* Campe, Julius
Hoffmann, Ernst Theodor Amadeus, 25, 53

Hoffmann von Fallersleben, August Heinrich, 101
Hofrichter, Laura, 155n6, 157n8
Homer, 28, 3 (*Odyssey*), 37 (*Iliad*)
Housman, A.E., 157n7
Hugo, Victor Maria, 10

Ibsen, Henrik, 56
Irving, Washington, 31

Jean Paul (Jean Paul Friedrich Richter), 53
Jones, Howard Mumford, 152n7
Jung, Carl Gustav, 48, 68, 145, 158n13
Jung Deutschland (Young Germany), 10, 58, 64

Kafka, Franz, 89, 119, 122, 155n7, 156n22
Kämmerling, Bernd, 158n22
Kant, Immanuel, 33, 49, 50, 51
Karpeles, Gustav, 153n4
Kaufmann, Hans, 114
Kircher, Hartmut, 155n12
Klopstock, Friedrich Gottlieb, 28
Kolb, Gustav, 109
Kollwitz, Käthe, 134
Koopmann, Helmut, 152n6, 153n4, 154n12, 155n5, 157n29, 158n16
Kraus, Karl, 147, 148, 158n21, 158n22
Kreutzer, Leo, 153n1, 153n2, 155n8
Krinitz, Elise ("La Mouche"), alias Camille Selden, 138

Lamartine, Alphonse de, 109, 110
Laube, Heinrich, 56, 64, 71
Lehrer, Tom, 124
Leppmann, Wolfgang, 153n4

Lessing, Gotthold Ephraim, 49, 52, 70
Lewald, Fanny, 151n2
Lindner, Friedrich Georg Ludwig, 7
Liptzin, Sol, 153n4, 157n6, 157n8, 157n10
Liszt, Franz, 10
Loeb, Ernst, 151n6, 155n12, 157n8, 157n9
Loeben, Otto Heinrich von, 20
Loewenthal, Erich, 152n2
Louis XVI, King of France, 153n5
Louis Philippe, King of the French (Citizen-King), 1, 9, 45, 46, 108
Ludwig, Emil, 148
Lumley, Benjamin, 71
Luther, Martin, 49, 143, 144, 145, 156n25

Maché, Ulrich, 153n4
Mann, Thomas, 56, 63, 65, 153n9
Marx, Karl, 46, 48, 79, 92, 107, 145, 151n6, 153n4
Mascagni, Pietro, 71
Massmann, Hans Ferdinand, 8
Mayer, Hans, 158n18
Meissner, Alfred, 109
Menzel, Wolfgang, 55, 153n7
Metternich, Klemens Wenzel Lothar, Prince, 1, 7, 39, 44, 64
Minnesänger, 26, 101
Molière (Jean Baptiste Poquelin), 53
Mosse, George L., 158n17
Mozart, Wolfgang Amadeus, 41
Mundt, Theodor, 64
Muschg, Walter, 158n20
Musset, Alfred de, 10

Napoleon I, Emperor of the French, 1, 2, 6, 13, 14, 35, 37, 38, 39, 59, 109, 151n1, 152n7

Napoleon III, (Charles) Louis, 109
Nerval, Girard de, 10
Nietzsche, Friedrich, 48, 49, 56, 63, 82, 145, 146, 147, 158n14, 158n19
Nostiz, Count, 138
Novalis (Friedrich Leopold von Hardenberg), 53

Paganini, Nicolò, 65
Palmer, R.R., 155n8
Petronius, Arbiter, 99
Philistine, 3, 8, 32–35, 36, 42, 67, 133, 144
Platen–Hallermünde, August, Count, 8, 41, 55
Plato, 54
Politzer, Heinz, 157n8
Ponce de Leon, Juan, 140
Prawer, S.S., 154n4, 156n18, 157n8
Prussia, Prussian, 2, 5, 10, 74, 78, 80, 83, 85, 107

Reeves, Nigel, 157n8
Religion, 2, 27, 28, 35, 36, 37, 40, 42, 49, 50, 51, 70, 73, 110–14, 128
Richter, Karl, 154n2
Ringelnatz, Joachim (Hans Bötticher), 124
Rippmann, Inge, 153n10
Robespierre, Maximilian de, 45, 58
Rogge, Friedrich Wilhelm, 157n2
Rose, William, 155n12, 157n8
Rosenthal, Ludwig, 155n12
Rothschild, James Mayer, Baron de, 10, 59
Rousseau, Jean Jacques, 46
Ruge, Arnold, 92, 151n6

Saint-Simon, Claude Henri de Rouvroy, Comte de, and Saint-

Simonian concepts, 6, 9, 36, 48, 94, 99
Salinger, Herman, 157n7
Sammons, Jeffrey L., 151n6, 152n8, 154n12, 155n1, 155n12, 157n30, 157n8, 159n26
Sand, George (Lucile-Aurore Dupin Dudevant), 10
Sandor, A.I., 157n8
Schallmeyer, Agidius Jakob, 2
Schelling, Friedrich, 51, 74, 105, 154n1
Schenk, Eduard von, 7
Schiller, Friedrich, 28, 53
Schlegel, August Wilhelm, 4, 53, 55
Schlegel, Friedrich, 53
Schubert, Franz, 25
Schumann, Robert, 13
Schwab-Felisch, H., 156n27
Schweickert, Alexander, 157n12
Scott, Sir Walter, 35, 66
Sensualism and Spiritualism, 35, 52, 55, 56, 58, 59, 62, 67, 71, 99, 100, 114, 119–22
Sethe, Christian, 2, 3
Shakespeare, William, 57, 60, 70 (Romeo and Juliet), 78, 154n11
Signatur des Geistes, 5, 31, 39, 44, 45
Silcher, Friedrich, 20, 22
Simon, Ernst, 155n12
Spann, Meno, 157n8
Spontini, Gasparo, 33
Staël, Anne Louise Germaine de, 47, 53
Steen, Jan, 67, 68
Stendhal (Henri Beyle), 156n21
Stern, J.P., 157n8
Sternberger, Dolf, 151n6, 152n10, 155n5, 155n12

Sterne, Laurence, 31
Stimmungsbrechung, 23–29
Storz, Gerhard, 26, 152n5, 158n24
Strauss, Richard, 78
Strauss, Salomon, 11, 56, 152n11

Tabak, Israel, 157n8
Tieck, Johann Ludwig, 10, 28, 45, 53

Uhland, Ludwig, 10, 53
Unzer, Gustav Friedrich von, 152n1

Varnhagen von Ense, Karl August, 5, 7, 8
Varnhagen von Ense, Rahel (née Levin), 5, 8
Victor, Walther, 155n8
Voltaire (François Marie Arouet), 46
Vorwärts! 79, 92, 134

Wadepuhl, Walter, 153n4
Wagner, Richard, 54, 69, 117
Walther von der Vogelweide, 101
Weigand, Hermann J., 155n12, 157n8
Weiberg, Kurt, 154n3, 157n4, 157n8, 158n13
Weinbarg, Ludolf, 64
Wilde, Oscar, 78
William II, German Emperor, 156n27
Windfuhr, Manfred, 151n6, 152n6, 155n8
Wohl, Jeanette, 56, 152n11

Zeitgeist (spirit of the age). *See Signatur des Geistes*
Zerrissenheit, 36, 37
Zweig, Stefan, 148, 158n23

831.7
H468

114905